the BRANDED

COOKBOOK

Limited

Nick Sandler & Johnny Acton

FOR THE WORLD'S FAVOURITE FOOD BRANDS

Dedicated to

Luke

First published in Great Britain in 2008 by
Kyle Cathie Limited
122 Arlington Road
London NW1 7HP
general.enquiries@kyle-cathie.com
www.kylecathie.com

10 9 8 7 6 5 4 3 2 1

ISBN 978-1-85626-776-2

Text © 2008 Nick Sandler and
Johnny Acton

Photography © 2008 Jonathan Gregson
(see also additional copyright
acknowledgements on page 160)

Book design © 2008 Jake Tilson Studio

Project editor: Jennifer Wheatley
Designer: Jake Tilson Studio
Photographer: Jonathan Gregson
Home economy: Linda Tubby
Styling: Tabitha Hawkins
Picture research: Vicki Murrell
Copy editor: Jane Bamforth
Production director: Sha Huxtable

Nick Sandler and Johnny Acton are hereby
identified as the authors of this work in
accordance with Section 77 of the Copyright,
Designs and Patents Act 1988.

A Cataloguing In Publication record for this
title is available from the British Library.

All the brands featured in this book are
registered trade marks of their owners.
See page 160 for individual
acknowledgements.

Kyle Cathie Ltd is not connected in any
way to the brands or their owners.

The Authors

Nick Sandler is the Creative Chef
for Pret A Manger, and therefore
responsible for countless lunches on
a daily basis. He is also a freelance
development chef, creating new
dishes for delis and supermarkets.

Johnny Acton is a writer and journalist
who has authored books on topics
ranging from the role of high altitude
ballooning in the Space Race (*The Man
Who Touched the Sky*) to the history
of money (*Minted*).

Together Nick and Johnny have written
four books for Kyle Cathie Ltd – *Soup,
Mushroom, Preserved* and *Duchy
Originals Cookbook*.

CONTENTS

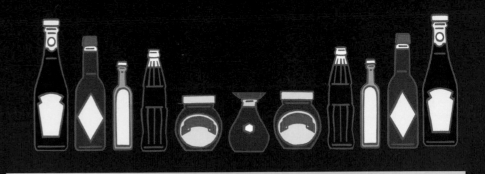

INTRODUCTION

Where would we be without cornflakes, peanut butter and ketchup? Our guess is that we would be in a much duller world.

Look into a food cupboard anywhere on earth. You are almost guaranteed to find some and possibly all of the following products: Kellogg's cornflakes, Nutella, Hellmann's mayonnaise, Lea & Perrins Worcestershire sauce, Tabasco pepper sauce and Heinz baked beans.

The idea at the heart of *The Branded Cookbook* is that these and similar items have not stood the tests of time and geography because people are duped by marketing. It's because they are extremely good.

And we want to explode the myth that the great food brands are just for the lazy and uncreative. As this book aims to prove, they can be used to make delicious, inventive dishes that are accessible to almost everyone. All that is needed is an adventurous spirit and a bit of imagination.

The Philosophy of *The Branded Cookbook*

The world's great food brands hold a special place in our hearts. They are comforting, familiar and have such vivid identities that we form strong emotional attachments to them. They loom large in our childhood memories and many of them attract cult followings. They are also part of our shared experience. In short, they make us feel nostalgic and safe.

Healthy and organic foods are rightly winning the battle for dominance on our plates, a development which we have long championed. But, as ever in the backlash against outdated and harmful eating practices, there is a danger of going too far in the other direction. Many largely unquestioned myths have arisen about global brands (see 'The Advantages of Branded Food' below)

and we see it as our job to challenge them. Beyond myth-busting, we are frankly tired of culinary Puritanism. We don't want to be lambasted for liking a bit of ketchup on our shepherd's pie. We should eat healthily, yes, but our motto is that food should be about enjoyment. In the long run, eating for pleasure is likely to prove a lot healthier than turning it into a guilt-fest. When you come down to it, few of the best things in life are strictly necessary. Your body won't starve if you deny yourself treats, but your spirit just might.

Another consideration is practicality. The big brands are readily available just about everywhere and, as mentioned, you almost certainly have several of them in your larder. The question then becomes how to use them to make delicious and interesting dishes.

Finally, the stories of the great food brands are fascinating in themselves. One of the chief aims of this book is to reveal the magic in ingredients we might be tempted to take for granted. Cornflakes suddenly become a lot more interesting when we find out that they were invented as part of a diet designed by Seventh Day Adventists to 'dampen the animal passions'. Similarly, adding a splash of Kikkoman to a dish becomes

more of an event once you are aware the 'Sun King' Louis XIV was a big fan of soy sauce in general and very probably of that particular brand.

The History of Branded Food

According to *The Guinness Book of Records,* the world's oldest brand is Lyle's Golden Syrup, a by-product of the sugar refining industry first sold in 1885. We respectfully beg to differ. Our definition of what constitutes a brand may be somewhat looser (we allow substantial changes in packaging), but as far as we are concerned Guinness itself is over a hundred years older. But even the 'Irish champagne' is a stripling compared with the most ancient brand we have come across. That honour goes to Liubiju, a pickle manufacturer based in Beijing and well known to residents of the city. A recently discovered title deed shows that the firm was sold to a family named Zhao in the ninth year of the reign of the Emperor Jiajing, in other words in 1530! Chinese pickles aside, *The Guinness Book of Records* is right to the extent that most of the world's great food brands date from the 19th century. The reason for this can be expressed in two words: Industrial Revolution. In order

for the big brands to develop and take root, the manufacturers needed the following conditions in place:

✻ Large urban populations in no position to grow their own food.

✻ Mechanised manufacturing methods allowing the production and packaging of large quantities of consistent food.

✻ Efficient transport links enabling national and international distribution.

✻ Printing techniques, media and literacy advanced enough to permit mass advertising.

By the late Victorian era, the ground was well prepared. The main challenges facing the brand pioneers were getting people to recognise their products and to trust them. The first need spawned a new kind of advertising industry. Memorable logos were designed, many of which are still with us today, while copywriters busied themselves creating attention-grabbing advertisements with catchy slogans. As far as establishing trust was concerned, the new brands were aided by the often dubious quality of the food available before their appearance. Adulteration with various fillers was commonplace, spoilage was

a major problem and badly canned or bottled foods could be downright dangerous. In contrast, the brand manufacturers could offer safe, consistent, nasty-free products with long shelf lives. They also freed their customers from the burden of making everything from scratch from the raw materials. Convenience was a major selling point. When Heinz tomato ketchup was launched in 1876, for example, it was billed as 'A blessed relief for Mother and other women in the household!'.

During the 20th and early 21st centuries, brands proliferated to such an extent that there are now tens of thousands of branded products available in the average supermarket. Nevertheless, many have fallen along the wayside. The survival of the 17 brands featured in this book, whose ages range from 60 years to 300 plus, is proof of their enduring appeal.

The Advantages of Branded Food

The big food brands have had an unfair press in recent years. Take the widespread assumption that they are necessarily bad for you. In fact, most manufacturers have taken on board

contemporary dietary concerns by reducing the salt and sugar contents of their products, often dramatically. Meanwhile, a brief glance at history (see above) reveals that the most successful brands represent a considerable improvement on what went before. Similarly, the notions that they are invariably produced exploitatively and without regard to the environment are just plain wrong. Many were founded on and maintain admirable philanthropic principles, and most of the brands covered in this book are now available in organic form. The moral of the story is this: there's no need to throw the baby out with the bath water. It's time for a rethink.

All the brands featured in this book have unique flavours, textures or both. They have distinctive personalities, visually, historically and taste-wise. They are ubiquitous, affordable and have long shelf lives, so they are easy to obtain and to store. They are versatile and save time, so incorporating them into your recipes is a doddle. Above all, they are consistent. When you buy a bottle of Tabasco pepper sauce or a packet of Kellogg's cornflakes you know exactly what you are getting, whether you shop in Birmingham, Baltimore or Bombay.

✱✱✱✱✱✱✱✱ ✱✱✱✱✱✱✱✱✱✱✱✱✱✱✱✱✱✱✱✱ ✱✱✱✱✱✱✱✱✱✱✱✱✱✱✱

Brand Selection

Although all the brands featured in this book can fairly be described as 'big', we haven't picked them purely on the basis of size. Nor, in case there are any sceptics out there, has our choice been influenced by financial incentives (we wish!). *The Branded Cookbook,* then, is not a series of glorified advertisements. It's more a collection of hymns of praise to the featured products.

When selecting the brands to be included in this book, our criteria have been as follows:

✱ **Quality**

Although these things are inevitably subjective, we've always tried to go for 'best of breed'.

✱ **Popularity**

We've picked the most popular brands (some verging on the cultish) because they are the ones you are most likely to want to cook with. There's also a good chance you already have them around the house.

✱ **Distinctiveness**

The chosen brands tend to be either quite unlike anything else (Camp coffee) or to have certain qualities that elevate them above their competitors.

✱ **Good Stories**

We like brands with interesting histories behind them.

✱ **Versatility**

This being a recipe book, the most useful brands are those with multiple culinary applications. Our favourites have a place in sweet, savoury, oriental and traditional British cookery alike.

✱ **Difficult to Duplicate**

Most of our big 17 are formulas rather than single ingredient affairs. (The obvious exception is Quaker oats, which we've included precisely because of the company's remarkable achievement in branding something generic, namely oats). You are unlikely to have the time, patience or know-how to knock up your own Worcestershire sauce or Coca-Cola. Even if you did, they probably wouldn't be as good as the originals. The makers of our chosen brands have had decades and sometimes centuries to perfect their arts. Many of the products hinge on complex industrial processes – just try making cream cheese at home – and in any case the manufacturers wisely tend to keep their recipes secret.

✱ **Idiosyncratic Personal Preference**

We're well aware that most of the brands in this book have rivals with merits of their own. We've just picked the ones that we like the best or reckon are the most definitive. We're certainly not about to browbeat you if you happen to prefer Pepsi to Coke or Sunpat peanut butter to Skippy. Fortunately, you can easily substitute similar brands for the ones specified in the recipes.

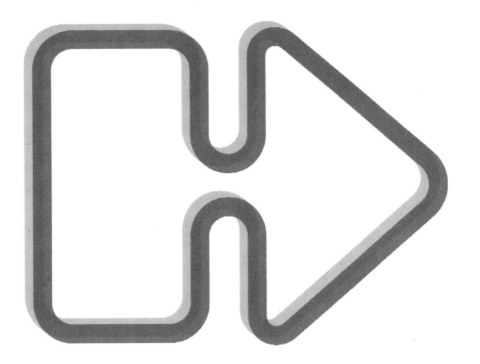

The Recipes

In choosing the recipes for this book we have been guided by a simple principle. In a nutshell, we want to show you how 'unglamorous' branded ingredients can be used to make delicious dishes that neither cost an arm or a leg nor demand that you're a cordon bleu chef. The recipes in *The Branded Cookbook* are sometimes surprising and always scrumptious. They vary from the simple to the reasonably ambitious, but none of them require unusual ingredients or entail much faffing around. Students, housewives and foodies alike should find plenty to suit them. Some recipes are for 'classics', others are for less obvious dishes like stir-fried pork with Hellmann's mayonnaise and oyster sauce. We hope that they will open your mind to the creative possibilities of even the most familiar ingredients.

KELLOGG'S CORNFLAKES

Nature's traditional alarm clock was the crowing of a cockerel. A good proportion of the world's population still wake up to a rooster, but this one is two dimensional.

His name is Cornelius and since 1958 he has adorned the packaging of Kellogg's cornflakes, the most popular breakfast cereal on Earth.

Over the years, the genius of Kellogg's advertising has been to forge two associations in peoples' minds. The first is between cornflakes and getting up in the morning, hence Cornelius. This makes them the obvious candidate for breakfast (the following recipes will show that they can play starring roles in other meals as well). The second connection is with the sun, which makes cornflakes an obvious source of energy. Helped by the golden colour of the flakes themselves, the message that comes across is that these crispy shards of rolled maize are solar rays solidified. Throw in their convenience and deliciousness and you have a product that is present in the larders of almost half the households in the country at any given time.

Given their popularity, you might expect cornflakes to have been specifically designed as a breakfast cereal. In fact, they came into existence by accident. Their creators were John Harvey Kellogg and his brother William Keith, a pair of Seventh Day Adventists who ran a health clinic in Michigan. Treatment at the

Battle Creek Sanitarium was based on the dietary principles established by Sylvester Graham, the inventor of Graham crackers and a passionate advocate of vegetarianism and sexual abstinence. Patients were encouraged to take part in chaste fresh-air activities and were prescribed bland, low-protein diets based on grains. One day in 1894, the Kellogg brothers cooked up a batch of wheat, forgot about it and returned to find that it had gone stale. Being thrifty folk, they attempted to salvage the situation by converting the wheat into bread. When they passed it through a rolling machine, however, what emerged was not the expected sheet of dough but little flakes. Still not prepared to give up on the wheat, they toasted the flakes and fed them to their patients with milk and marshmallows. They went down a storm. Soon, departing residents were requesting packets of the new cereal to take home with them.

Excited by their discovery, the Kellogg brothers filed a patent for the production of what they initially called 'Granose' and started to experiment with other grains, eventually settling on maize as the source of the tastiest flakes. William also took to adding malted barley during the pre-toasting steaming phase, which

added a crucial new element to the flavour. In 1906, he decided to devote himself to cornflakes full time. He left the sanitarium, set up the Kellogg Company and added sugar to the recipe to make the product still more appealing. His brother never forgave him for this betrayal of Battle Creek principles, but the public voted with their wallets.

As anyone who has left a bowl of Kellogg's cornflakes soaking in milk for any length of time knows, their chief charm is their crunchiness. Take that away and they become, well, soggy. (Nick actually rather likes soggy cornflakes but he's an eccentric.) As a result, successful cornflake recipes are those in which their original, dry texture is maintained. The quintessential example is the flapjack, that staple of village fetes and home economics lessons. As there's a fair chance you have either overdosed on flapjacks à la cornflake or know how to make them already, we haven't included them here. Instead, we present a handful of less obvious dishes in which the key is the crunch.

1960s magazine advert.

One o'clock, a summer's night,
Time for Kellogg's, crisp and light,
Pour the milk, so sparkling white–
Who can wait till breakfast?

(To the tune of Kellogg's "Sunshine" TV commercial)

Kellogg's CORN FLAKES

There's 140 days of sunshine in a box of Kellogg's Corn Flakes

Kellogg's CORN FLAKES *The Sunshine Breakfast*

FRIED CHICKEN WITH SOUTHERN CORNFLAKE CRUMB

1946 cornflakes packet.

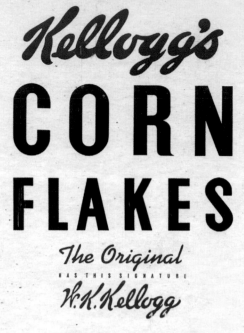

Banish all thoughts of Colonels and stripy tubs from your mind and treat yourself to some homemade southern fried chicken. Serve with French fries and a crisp salad.

Serves 2

For the crumb

50g Kellogg's cornflakes

1 teaspoon Maldon sea salt

½ teaspoon white pepper

2 teaspoons dried onion flakes

1 teaspoon paprika

1 teaspoon dried mixed herbs

1 teaspoon Colman's mustard powder

½ teaspoon ground cumin

½ teaspoon ground allspice

For the chicken

2 chicken breasts or boneless thighs, cut into strips

2 tablespoons plain flour

1 large egg, lightly beaten

500ml vegetable oil, for deep-frying

To make the chicken coating, combine the crumb ingredients in a small bowl and scrunch up with your fingers until the cornflakes have disintegrated into coarse crumbs.

Take the chicken strips and shake them around in the flour until coated. Lay each chicken strip individually into the beaten egg, then lift into the crumb and coat evenly.

In a large saucepan heat up the oil to approximately 160°C/325°F and deep-fry the chicken for 5–7 minutes until golden brown.

CORNFLAKE CAKES

We planned to use standard plain chocolate for this recipe but Nick made it with a luxury brand called Valrhona by mistake. As a result, the flavour of the chocolate came through particularly strongly. Conclusion: use a cheap dark chocolate and these cakes will be fine; use a gourmet dark chocolate and they will be food for the gods. You will need some paper cake cases.

Makes 12

50g unsalted butter, finely diced
3 tablespoons golden syrup
100g plain chocolate
100g Kellogg's cornflakes
Chocolate strands, to decorate (optional)

Place the butter, golden syrup and plain chocolate in a large bowl. Heat for about 1 minute in the microwave. The butter should be almost melted, so stir it in until you have a glossy, smooth mixture.

Add the cornflakes and gently stir with a spatula, trying not to break the cornflakes as you do so. The stirring will take a couple of minutes before all the cornflakes are coated.

Spoon into the cake cases until each one is bursting with chocolate-coated cornflakes.

For an extra chocolate fix, these are very nice sprinkled with chocolate strands.

Chill in the fridge for an hour until set and then store in an airtight container in a cool place for up to a week.

KELLOGG'S CORNFLAKE AND PEANUT BUTTER BROKEN BARS

The shops are heaving with power bars, health bars, breakfast bars and various other bars designed for when you don't have time to eat a proper meal. Why not make your own? They are a fraction of the price, store well and are scrummy.

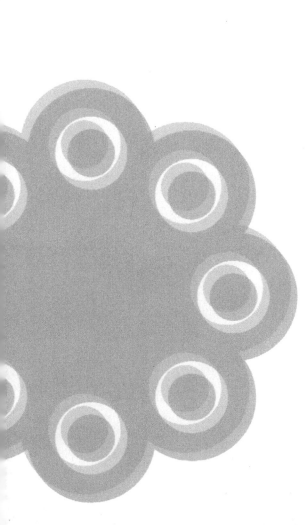

Serves 4

> 150g peanuts, skin off or on
> 125g Kellogg's cornflakes
> 4 heaped tablespoons Skippy smooth peanut butter
> 5 tablespoons maple syrup
> Butter, for greasing

Preheat the oven to 180°C/350°F/gas mark 4. Grease a baking tray with a little butter, then line it with greaseproof paper.

Mix up the ingredients in a large bowl using your fingers. Make sure you scrunch them up well.

Tamp down the mixture in the tray to the edges. You want it nice and firm and even. Bake in the oven for 15–20 minutes; it should be ever so slightly browned.

Take out of the oven and let cool for a few minutes, then turn out onto a chopping board. Ease the tin off, then gently peel away the greaseproof paper.

Wait until the tray bake is completely cool, then cut with a long, sharp knife into bars. Some will break but that's OK; you can call it munchy cornflake crunch or cornflake peanut brittle or maple flake delights, etc.

Store in an airtight container for up to 2 weeks.

CORNFLAKE MACAROONS

Macaroons are related to meringues, both being crunchy confections made with egg whites. They were traditionally flavoured with almond powder but dessicated coconut works at least as well.

Makes 10–12 macaroons

- 100g desiccated coconut, plus a little extra to roll the balls in
- 75g Kellogg's cornflakes
- 2 extra-large or 3 small egg whites
- 150g caster sugar
- 1 teaspoon vanilla extract
- Pinch of Maldon sea salt

Preheat the oven to 160°C/325°F/ gas mark 3.

Mix all the ingredients together in a large bowl with your fingers, crushing the cornflakes as you go.

Wash your hands, then with your fingers still damp firmly shape the mixture into golf ball-sized spheres. Roll each ball in a little desiccated coconut.

Bake in the oven for 20 minutes.

These light delights will store in an airtight container for a few days but they are best eaten on the day.

1938 cornflakes packet.

QUAKER OATS

Quaker oats are rather different from the other brands in this book in that they have only one ingredient and nothing much has been done to it, at least at first glance.

The oats are separated from any other material picked up during harvesting, their husks are removed and then they are steamed to bring out their flavour. Finally, they are cut into two or three pieces and rolled very thinly. That's about it. But it is precisely through perfecting a simple process that yields a consistent, reliable end product that the manufacturers have built their reputation. That and having a very good logo.

Try not to be shocked but Quaker oats have nothing to do with the Christian sect officially known as the Society of Friends. They are, however, exactly the kind of thing those sensible people are liable to eat. The name was chosen after one of the founding partners, Henry D Seymour of Ravenna, Ohio, read an encyclopaedia article about Quakers and realised that their values – honesty, integrity and simplicity – mirrored the message he wanted to get across about his oats. So he and his partner William Heston named their business The Quaker Mill Company. On September 4th 1877, they registered a full-length portrait of a Quaker man as a trademark, a first for an American breakfast cereal. He was holding a scroll inscribed with the word 'pure'. The image of the now-famous Quaker Man has been updated just three times, in 1946, 1957 and 1972.

In 1901, the Quaker Mill Company teamed up with two other Midwestern milling firms to form the Quaker Oats Company. One operated the largest cereal mill in the world in Cedar Rapids, Iowa; the other was the German Mills American Oatmeal Company of Ohio, founded by Ferdinand Schumacher, the 'Oatmeal King', in 1856. All three shared the aim of selling top-quality branded oats to save American housewives from the lottery of buying them from open barrels in grocery stores.

Oats were the last of the major grains to be domesticated and used to be regarded as a downmarket food suitable only for horses and (as far as the Romans and Englishmen with an anti-Scottish bent were concerned) barbarians. At the heart of the image problem was the fact that they quickly go rancid if they aren't processed properly. This is because they contain a small amount of fat, together with a fat-dissolving enzyme. By perfecting the milling process, the Quaker Oats Company opened up a huge new market. Another major boon was the discovery that oats actively lower body cholesterol. They had long been regarded as healthy but this property, which is shared by no other wholegrain, was the icing on the cake.

The obvious way to use Quaker oats is to make porridge. We're definitely in favour of that. In fact, Johnny once appeared on a BBC discussion programme to argue the merits of porridge over the fried breakfast served at the Savoy Hotel. But there are many other excellent ways of incorporating the oats into your cooking. They make wonderful crusty toppings for pies and can be used as a flavoursome alternative to breadcrumbs (see our fish finger recipe). Their slight chewiness works extremely well in cakes and biscuits, and you won't find a better health drink than Nick's Quaker oat and mango *vitamina*.

OATMEAL AND GUINNESS BREAD

This recipe makes a beautiful malty loaf. After it has cooled you may want to slice it and freeze it for toast. You will need a mixer with a dough hook and a large loaf tin, 24–26cm long and 6–8cm deep.

Makes 1 loaf

- **500g strong white bread flour**
- **1½ teaspoons dried yeast**
- **100g Quaker oats, plus extra for sprinkling**
- **2 heaped teaspoons Maldon sea salt**
- **500ml Guinness**

Place the flour, yeast, oats and salt in the food mixer bowl and mix around loosely with your fingers to distribute the yeast and salt. Add the Guinness and knead on low speed for 5 minutes, then let the dough rest in the bowl for 10 minutes.

Turn the dough out onto a lightly floured surface and fold it over itself a few times. Roll into a rough sausage and place in the loaf tin. Leave to rise in a warm place for 1½ hours, or until the dough has risen over the top of the tin.

After the dough has been rising for 1 hour, preheat the oven to 240°C/475°F/gas mark 9.

When the dough has risen nicely, sprinkle it with a thin layer of oats and shove it in the oven. After 10 minutes turn the temperature down to 220°C/425°F/gas mark 8 and bake for a further 20–25 minutes. Please note: do not open the oven during the first 10 minutes of cooking.

To see if the bread is ready, tap it with your fingers: if it sounds hollow it is ready. If you are not sure give the loaf a bit longer.

Advertisement on a trade card, circa 1890s.

QUAKER OAT PANCAKES WITH BACON AND MUSHROOM FILLING

* *

Food allergies seem to be becoming ever more common and one of the major allergens is wheat. Although the Quaker Oats Company cannot guarantee that traces of gluten haven't snuck into the product somewhere along the line, these delicious pancakes largely get round the problem as they are based on oats. You will need a 9–10cm pancake ring, for these are American-style pancakes, and a large non-stick pan or griddle.

Serves 4

150g Quaker oats
1 teaspoon baking powder
½ teaspoon Maldon sea salt
250ml whole milk
1 drop vanilla extract
50ml double cream
1 large egg, beaten
50g butter, melted
Vegetable oil, for frying
12 rashers streaky bacon
Butter, for frying
12 medium-sized mushrooms, sliced
Heinz tomato ketchup, to serve

Blend the oats in a food processor for 1 minute to make oatmeal.

Pour the oatmeal, baking powder and salt into a bowl and mix together. Add the milk, vanilla extract, double cream and egg. Whisk in thoroughly.

Finally, pour in the melted butter, whisking as you do so.

Heat up a large non-stick pan and swirl around about 1 tablespoon of vegetable oil. Pour enough batter into the pancake ring so that it flows to the sides. Cook over a low to medium heat for around 30 seconds until the pancake has firmed up a little, then remove the ring (with a cloth – it will be hot). Replace the ring

elsewhere in the pan and pour some more pancake mixture in. Repeat the process until the pan is full. Give each pancake 3–4 minutes on each side – it should be golden brown.

As you cook the pancakes pile them up on a plate by the hob to keep them warm. If you aren't going to be using them right away, they can be stored in the fridge and heated up in the microwave.

Gently fry the bacon in a pan until nice and crispy. Heat a blob of butter in another pan and fry the mushrooms.

You are now going to make a pancake sandwich. Place a pancake on a plate, top with 2 rashers of bacon, some sliced mushrooms and a generous squirt of ketchup. Finally, top with another pancake. Voila! Perfect for breakfast!

Oat and nut munch is baked in a shallow baking dish or on a baking sheet until it caramelises into a crunchy brittle. It is then broken into bite-sized pieces.

OAT AND NUT MUNCH

Serves 6

- 100g Quaker oats
- 50g whole almonds
- 50g cashew nuts
- 50g desiccated coconut
- 50g pecan nuts
- 25g soft brown sugar
- 75g golden syrup
- 1½ tablespoons vegetable oil
- 1 tablespoon clear honey

Preheat the oven to 160°C/325°F/ gas mark 3.

In a large bowl mix together the oats, almonds, cashew nuts, coconut, pecan nuts and sugar.

Gently heat the golden syrup, vegetable oil and honey together in a small saucepan.

Pour the liquid ingredients over the dry ingredients and mix together using a spatula until the mixture is gluey.

Spread to about 2cm thick on a baking tray and flatten. Bake for 35–40 minutes.

Check the nuts carefully towards the end of the cooking process to make sure they don't burn. If they are getting a little dark, cover with foil and turn the oven down a tad.

Push down any prominent nuts when you take it out of the oven. Leave to cool for a least half an hour, then break into bite-sized pieces.

This oaty munch can be stored for up to 4 weeks in an airtight container.

QUAKER OAT AND MANGO VITAMINA

A *vitamina* is a Brazilian drink based on oats and coconut. It's the breakfast drink that has everything. In Brazil they flavour it with a variety of tropical fruits. We've used mango, but you can use any soft fruit you fancy. You will need a hand blender.

Serves 2

1 banana, broken into pieces

1 medium mango, peeled and cut into small chunks

2 heaped tablespoons Quaker oats

100ml coconut milk

150g Greek yogurt

200ml semi-skimmed milk

Squeeze of fresh lime juice

Blend all the ingredients together until relatively smooth. The oats will add a grainy texture to the drink.

Drink immediately, or chill and drink within a couple of hours.

APPLE AND OAT CAKE SLICES WITH MARMALADE GLAZE

This deliciously fruity cake is moist and slightly tart. After it comes out of the oven you can cut it into bars or squares. They're great for packed lunches or picnics.

Bramley apples are used in the cake, but later on in the recipe a different type of apple is used. The reason for this is that Bramleys fall meltingly apart when cooked, whereas the eating apples, which are used for the topping, stay firm.

You will need a non-stick baking tray around 30 x 20cm for this cake.

Serves 8–10

- 100g unsalted butter
- 100g vegetable oil
- 150g golden caster sugar
- 3 large eggs, beaten
- 200g Bramley or other cooking apples, cut into chunks
- 100g raisins
- 100g ground almonds
- 100g self-raising flour
- 50g Quaker oats
- 1½ teaspoons baking powder
- 2 tablespoons maple syrup
- Juice of ½ lemon
- 4 large Jonagold, Braeburn or Golden Delicious apples, cored and thinly sliced
- 2 tablespoons marmalade (finely cut or thick cut – whichever you prefer)
- Butter, for greasing

Preheat the oven to 180°C/350°F/gas mark 4. Grease the baking tray with butter, then line it with greaseproof paper, letting the paper overlap the edges of the tin so you can lift the cake out when cooked.

In a small pan gently melt the butter. It should be warm but not hot.

Pour the butter into a mixing bowl with the oil and sugar. Gently beat with a wooden spoon for a few minutes.

Gradually add the egg, continuing to beat. Add the apple chunks, raisins, almonds, flour, oats, baking powder, maple syrup and lemon juice. Gently stir until the mixture is well combined, then pour into the prepared baking tray.

Arrange the apple slices over the top of the cake as shown in the picture. Melt the marmalade in a small saucepan, then brush the cake with the marmalade. Bake for 40 minutes or until the apples are golden and slightly crisp. Let cool in the tray for 10 minutes or so, then lift out onto a wire rack to cool before slicing.

SALMON FISH CAKES WITH AN OATY CRUST

* *

Oats make a nice change from breadcrumbs as a coating for fish cakes and many other things besides. They provide a distinctive texture, a slight nuttiness and they feel healthier. Hellmann's mayo and Heinz tomato ketchup are essential for dipping. For this recipe you will need a large frying pan.

Makes about 8 fish cakes

3 medium-size potatoes, roughly diced

250g salmon, skinned and cut into small chunks

2 egg yolks

25g butter

Small handful of flat-leaf parsley, roughly chopped

Salt and freshly ground black pepper

100g Quaker oats

Vegetable oil, for frying

Bring a medium pan of water to the boil and cook the diced potatoes for 15–20 minutes or until soft. Drain.

Add the salmon, egg yolks, butter, parsley and seasoning to the potatoes in the pan. Mash all the ingredients with a potato masher until well combined.

Pour the oats onto a worksurface or large chopping board. Using a tablespoon, portion out a blob of mixture and spoon it into the oats. Remember, the salmon mixture is very soft, so the first thing you must do is sprinkle some oats on top and then gently squeeze the oats into it. Lift the fish cake from the oat pile, cradling it carefully in your hand. Repeat with the rest of the fish mixture.

Pour half a centimetre of vegetable oil into a large frying pan. Shallow-fry the fish cakes in two batches over a medium heat for 5 minutes on each side, until golden brown.

The key to this pie is the contrast between the creamy filling and the crispy topping. When you heat Quaker oats and grated cheese together, you end up with something with a splendidly crunchy texture. You will need a small baking dish for this recipe, ideally around 5cm deep and 25cm long.

FISHERMAN'S PIE WITH OATY CRUMBLE

Serves 4

For the mash

> 4 medium-size potatoes (about 200g each), each cut into 4 pieces
>
> 15g butter

For the filling

> 200g cooked frozen prawns
>
> 300g skinless boneless salmon, cut into chunks
>
> 200g trimmed asparagus spears, sliced
>
> 6 spring onions, sliced
>
> 200g crème fraîche
>
> Small sprig of flat-leaf parsley, roughly chopped
>
> Salt and freshly ground black pepper

For the crumble

> 100g mature Cheddar cheese, grated
>
> 50g Quaker oats

Preheat the oven to 180°C/350°F/ gas mark 4.

Bring a large pan of water to the boil and add the potatoes. Boil for 15–20 minutes, or until soft.

Place the prawns in the baking dish along with the salmon, asparagus, spring onions, crème fraîche and parsley. Season with black pepper and as much salt as you like. Then mix the contents of the dish together.

Drain the cooked potatoes, then add the butter and mash. Season with a little salt and pepper. Spread the mash on top of the fish mixture.

To make the crumble, place the grated Cheddar and the oats in a small bowl and mix them together with the tips of your fingers. Sprinkle the mixture on the pie and bake for 45–50 minutes.

NUTELLA

Necessity is the mother of invention, as the proverb goes, and the creation of Nutella was a case in point.

During the 1940s, when chocolate was in short supply in Europe as a result of World War II rationing, a pastry maker from the town of Alba in Piedmont in northern Italy had an ingenious idea. Why not eke out the cocoa that was available with something locally abundant and delicious like hazelnuts? So Pietro Ferrero used the nuts rather as the makers of Camp coffee had used chicory (see page 150), namely to render a luxury item affordable. In the process, he came up with a product that many preferred to the original, i.e. chocolate.

Ferrero's original chocolate and hazelnut concoction was called Pasta Gianduja. Gianduja is a jolly Piedmontese carnival character with a tricorn hat and a little upturned pigtail. Pasta in this context means 'paste', but Nutella's immediate ancestor was actually sold in block form. The idea was for customers to cut off slices and serve them on bread. In practice, however, they tended not to bother with the bread. This led Ferrero to introduce a spreadable version known as Supercrema Gianduja. It was a sixth of the price of regular chocolate, and through skilful marketing there was no need to wait until you had saved up enough money to buy an entire jar: shopkeepers were encouraged to sell single servings of Supercrema Gianduja from reusable branded glasses that are now collectors' items. An entire generation of Italian children grew up with the habit of popping into the local shop for a 'smear' on a piece of bread brought in for the purpose.

For several years, Supercrema Gianduja remained an Italian secret, but in 1964 Pietro Ferrero's son Michele decided that the time was right to unleash it on the rest of Europe. The paste, which was rebranded as Nutella, reached America in the 1980s and is now sold in more than 100 countries. According to the company literature, it outsells all brands of peanut butter combined.

For many, the sensory pleasures of Nutella verge on the indecent. This was picked up by the Italian actor/director Nanni Moretti. In a legendary scene from his film *Bianca* (1984), the hero (played by Moretti) wakes up in a sexual frenzy that he can only quench by scoffing an enormous jar of Nutella in bed. And there are no plans to tamper with the recipe. Many of the brands featured in this book have bowed to modern trends by producing diet versions. Not Ferrero. The idea of 'Nutella Lite' would horrify even the most weight-conscious fans of the spread, who find it perfect just the way it is.

It will come as no surprise that the recipes that follow lie on the dessert end of the spectrum. All of them make full use of Nutella's creamy chocolatiness and the roasted nut flavour that has enchanted the planet.

NUTELLA TRUFFLES

These are Nick's version of those famous gold-wrapped chocolates suitable for an ambassador. He's not being quite as clever as he thinks as those chocs are made by the same company that manufactures Nutella.

Makes about 12

> 4 ice-cream wafers
>
> 2 tablespoons almonds
>
> 3 tablespoons whole blanched hazelnuts
>
> 2 tablespoons Nutella

Preheat the oven to 180°C/350°F/ gas mark 4.

Using your fingers, crumble the ice-cream wafers until they are the size of large breadcrumbs.

Bake the almonds and hazelnuts in the oven for 8 minutes. Let cool. Remove 1 tablespoon of whole hazelnuts to be used later in the recipe. Process the remaining nuts in a food processor until finely ground.

Mix the ground almonds and hazelnuts and half the crumbled ice-cream wafers with the Nutella in a bowl. It will turn into silken chocolate praline.

Put the remaining crumbled wafers in a small bowl.

Pick up a blob of the truffled chocolate with a teaspoon and press in a whole roasted hazelnut until enveloped. Then place in the bowl of wafer crumbs and roll the truffle around until it is nicely coated with an even crunchy layer. Repeat to make around 12 truffles.

Store the truffles in the fridge to keep them firm. They should keep for a couple of weeks in an airtight container.

Nick's friends' daughters, Jessica and Amelia, were extremely disappointed when they came round with their parents for lunch to find there was no dessert. Nick explained that he'd been working hard on this book and hadn't had time to make anything.

'But how do you write a recipe?' asked Amelia, 'it must be really difficult'. He told them that it was. He explained that compiling the recipes involved a lot of travel, sometimes as far as the local supermarket. They looked suitably impressed.

'Would you like Nutella brownies with ice cream for dessert?' he enquired. 'Well, we'll have to create the recipe first'. This recipe is dedicated to Jessica (12) and Amelia (10).

You will need a 30 x 20cm baking tray.

NUTELLA BROWNIES

Makes 12

- 125g butter, plus extra for greasing
- 100g soft light brown sugar
- 400g jar Nutella
- 100ml double cream
- 2 large eggs, beaten
- 100g self-raising flour
- 100g ground almonds
- 1 teaspoon baking powder

Preheat the oven to 180°C/350°F/gas mark 4. Grease the baking tray and line with greaseproof paper.

Place the butter in a large bowl and heat gently in the microwave until just melted.

Whisk the sugar into the softened butter. Stir in the Nutella and the double cream using a wooden spoon.

Whisk in the eggs until incorporated and then stir in the flour, almonds and baking powder. Mix until smooth. Transfer into the baking tray using a spatula.

Bake for 20–25 minutes. Remove from the oven and either eat warm from the tin, or allow to cool, then transfer to a chopping board and slice into squares.

The brownies can be stored for a week in an airtight container. Amelia and Jessica will tell you that they are delicious warm with vanilla ice cream.

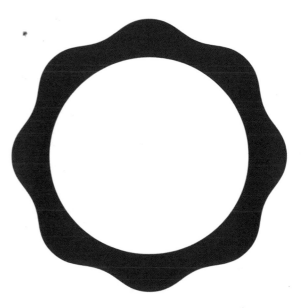

MOLTEN NUTELLA MUFFINS

These moreish muffins are best eaten when still slightly warm, perhaps with a dollop of ice cream. For this recipe you will need paper muffin cases and a shallow muffin tin.

Makes 4–5 medium muffins

- 100g unsalted butter
- 150g Nutella, at room temperature
- 2 large eggs
- 50g soft brown sugar
- 150g self-raising flour
- 400g jar Nutella, chilled

Preheat the oven to 180°C/350°F/ gas mark 4.

Place the butter and 150g Nutella in a small bowl, and heat briefly in the microwave until the butter is almost melted. Stir the butter and Nutella together until silky smooth.

In a medium-size bowl, mix the eggs, brown sugar and self-raising flour together using a wooden spoon. It will turn into a gloopy paste. Slowly pour in the Nutella and butter mixture, stirring as you go, to form a nice smooth batter. Spoon into the muffin cases. This will be messy. Use a spoon and your fingers to work it in.

Now take the jar of Nutella out of the fridge. It will have firmed up. Scoop a heaped teaspoon of the Nutella, spoon into the top of each muffin and press down into the mixture until it is just below the surface.

Bake the muffins for 18–20 minutes, until risen and cracked on top.

Up to 12 servings per jar.

BANOFFEE PIE WITH NUTELLA

This recipe works best with thoroughly ripe bananas. You will need a pie dish that's around 20cm wide and 6–8cm deep. This pie can also be made a day in advance and chilled overnight in the fridge.

Serves 4

2 tablespoons soft brown sugar

2 tablespoons dark rum

6 medium-size bananas, roughly sliced

4 heaped tablespoons Nutella

250ml double cream

397g tin of Carnation Caramel (or use *dulce de leche*)

Mix the sugar and rum together in a frying pan, then warm over a gentle heat for a couple of minutes.

Add the banana slices and fry for 5 minutes over a medium heat, stirring occasionally until the bananas become slightly mushy. Pour into the pie dish and use the back of a spoon to flatten them into an even layer.

Pour the double cream into a bowl and whisk with an electric hand whisk until it is just starting to thicken but still runny (it shouldn't be too thick).

Spoon the Nutella into a large bowl and heat in the microwave briefly, to soften it a touch. Add the Carnation Caramel and mix together thoroughly with a spoon. Pour in the whipped double cream and gently stir in. The mixture will become all swirly-whirly as the ingredients mix together. Try not to overmix. Pour the creamy mixture over the banana layer and let cool in the fridge for an hour or so before you serve.

CHOCOLATE LOG WITH NUTELLA

If you have any children to hand, enlist their help to decorate this fine chocolate log. They can really go to town with chocolate shavings, vermicelli, chocolate drops, Smarties and the like.

For this recipe you'll need a shallow oven tray around 30 x 40cm, but don't worry if it is a few cm off. You will also need some greaseproof paper, a tea towel and a food mixer or an electric hand whisk.

Serves 6–8

For the sponge

> 4 medium eggs
>
> 200g caster sugar
>
> Finely grated zest of 2 oranges
>
> 25g cocoa powder
>
> 100g self-raising flour
>
> Butter, for greasing

For the filling

> 300g Nutella
>
> 150ml thick double cream
>
> 200g Philadelphia cream cheese
>
> 1 tablespoon clear honey
>
> 2 tablespoons orange juice

To decorate

> Chocolate shavings (use a potato peeler), vermicelli, chocolate drops or Smarties

Preheat the oven to 180°C/350°F/gas mark 4. Grease the oven tray and line it with greaseproof paper.

Place the eggs and half the sugar in the food mixer bowl, or a large bowl, and whisk together for 5 minutes, or until they have increased 3 or 4 times in volume and are nice and frothy.

Add the orange zest and sift in the cocoa powder and flour. Sifting means shaking the cocoa and flour through a fine sieve to make them as fine as possible. A normal sieve will do if that's all you have. Mix all the ingredients together with a spatula but don't overmix or you will lose all the bubbles; don't undermix or you will have lumps of flour and cocoa.

Pour the mixture into the oven tray and level it off. Bake for around 10 minutes until the sponge feels firm and bouncy to the touch.

While the sponge is in the oven, run the cold tap over the tea towel and squeeze it out. Lay it onto the worksurface with the short end next to you.

Lay a sheet of greaseproof paper on top of the tea towel and press down. Sprinkle the greaseproof paper with caster sugar.

Take the sponge out of the oven and let it cool slightly, then turn it out onto the greaseproof paper. Roll it up tightly in the greaseproof paper (leave the tea towel behind). Cover with the wet tea towel until cool – about 40 minutes.

To make the filling, mix together all the ingredients except the orange juice in a bowl until smooth.

To assemble the log, unroll the sponge and sprinkle the orange juice on top. Spread the sponge with about half the filling then roll it up again. If you want to make a more authentic log shape, cut a piece off the end of the roll at an angle – this will become a knot in the wood.

Gently transfer the log to a serving plate or board, place the extra bit on the side and use a little of the filling to cement it to the log. Spread the outside with the rest of the filling.

Use a selection of your chosen decorations to make the finished log look really super-duper!

SKIPPY PEANUT BUTTER

There are several famous brands of peanut butter out there, but Skippy is the godfather of the genre and is, in our opinion, the best.

And in case you are confused by childhood memories of a TV programme based on the adventures of a certain bush kangaroo, it isn't Australian. It's American. Like Bill Clinton, Skippy peanut butter comes from Little Rock, Arkansas.

Here is something for people who look down on peanut butter to chew on. It was invented by a doctor from St Louis in 1890 as a dietary supplement for people with bad teeth. Indeed, most early versions of the spread were developed for medical purposes. Among those to get in on the act was John Harvey Kellogg of cornflakes fame (see page 12), who needed a high-protein vegetarian foodstuff for patients at his Michigan health clinic. In 1895, he and his brother William patented a process for producing 'a pasty adhesive substance that is for convenience of distinction termed nut butter.' Unfortunately it was rather bland, being made from steamed rather than roasted peanuts.

By the following decade, peanut butter, now typically made with roasted nuts, had escaped the confines of the medical world to become a mainstream product. The trouble was that the oily and solid components tended to separate. This problem was eventually solved by a Californian businessman called Joseph L Rosefield. In 1922, he patented a technique of making peanut butter that the scientifically minded may be interested to learn revolved around hydrogenation and the addition of an emulsifier. What matters to the rest of us is that it produced a non-separating spread with a shelf life of up to a year. And, unlike its gritty, sticky predecessors, the new version was deliciously creamy.

Rosefield initially licensed his invention to Swift & Company, the manufacturers of Peter Pan Peanut Butter, but in 1932 he started to make a version of his own. He gave it the brand name Skippy, a choice which embroiled his company in a protracted legal battle with Percy Crosby, the creator of an immensely popular cartoon strip that was also called Skippy. (It was about the adventures of a schoolboy named Skippy Skinner.) At one stage, Crosby's lawyers managed to invalidate Rosefield's trademark, but it was ultimately reinstated. Crosby's crusade was not aided by the fact that he ended up in an insane asylum, a development which rather took his eye off the ball. Ironically, his version of Skippy was a major influence on Charles M Schultz's Peanuts.

Today, around 90 million jars of Skippy are sold every year, making it the one of the most successful peanut butter brands in history. It is, of course, an obligatory ingredient in the PBJ ('peanut butter and jelly sandwich'), but its culinary uses extend way beyond the traditional American lunchbox. The wonderful thing about Skippy, and good peanut butter in general, is the way in which it coats the mouth with something with which it is very happy to be coated. It goes particularly well with spicy oriental dishes and makes an excellent saté sauce. You can also use it as the basis for some very fine soups.

Skippy is sold in both crunchy and smooth form. Both have their merits and both are absolutely packed with peanuts. On average, it takes 772 to make a 16.3oz jar.

SPICY PEANUT
SOUP

Peanut butter soups are big in West Africa and South East Asia. This one is great with loads of hot pitta bread.

Serves 4

2 tablespoons vegetable oil

2 medium-size carrots, roughly sliced

2 medium-size onions roughly diced

1 medium-size red chilli, roughly sliced

2 garlic cloves, roughly chopped

2cm piece fresh root ginger, sliced

2 teaspoons ground turmeric

1 tablespoon Marigold organic vegetable bouillon (our favourite)

1 teaspoon five-spice powder

2 medium-size potatoes, roughly diced

4 heaped tablespoons Skippy peanut butter

100ml coconut cream

2 teaspoons fish sauce (optional)

Small bunch of coriander, chopped

Juice of ½ lime

Heat the oil in the saucepan and fry the carrot, onion, red chilli, garlic, ginger and turmeric, covered, over a low-to-medium heat, stirring occasionally.

Add 800ml water, vegetable bouillon, five-spice powder and potatoes. Simmer for 20 minutes, until the potatoes are soft.

Add the peanut butter, coconut cream and fish sauce (if using). Blend until smooth. Add the chopped coriander and lime juice just before you take the saucepan off the heat.

Saté sauce is deservedly popular and easy to make if you have a jar of Skippy to hand. You will need some skewers.

SATÉ LAMB SKEWERS WITH PEANUT BUTTER

Serves 2

For the skewers

    1 tablespoon fish sauce

    1 tablespoon Tabasco pepper sauce

    Small handful of coriander, chopped

    Drop of vegetable oil

    2 spring onions, chopped

    400g lamb leg fillet, cubed

For the sauce

    2 tablespoons peanuts

    2 tablespoons Skippy peanut butter

    Juice of ½ lime

    1 tablespoon fish sauce

    ½ red chilli, chopped

    1 tablespoon Kikkoman soy sauce

    1 spring onion, sliced

    4 tablespoons water

    Lime wedges, to serve

Combine the fish sauce, Tabasco, coriander, vegetable oil and spring onions in a shallow dish. Add the lamb cubes and toss until coated, then marinate for at least an hour.

To make the sauce, dry fry the peanuts for 10–12 minutes over a relatively low heat until nicely browned, shaking around frequently. Let cool. Pulse in the blender until coarse. You could alternatively crush them with the flat of a knife, or a rolling pin, but be careful!

Combine all the sauce ingredients in a bowl.

When you are ready to cook, preheat the grill to medium. Thread 3 or 4 lamb cubes onto each skewer.

Grill the lamb for about 20 minutes, turning halfway. You can alternatively cook 'em up on the barbecue but don't cook for quite as long.

Serve the lamb with a little dipping dish of saté sauce and wedges of lime.

PAD THAI WITH SKIPPY PEANUT BUTTER

Pad Thai is the definitive Thai dish and surprisingly easy to make at home, provided you have a blender. Galangal is similar to fresh ginger but more aromatic. Look for it at Asian supermarkets.

Serves 2–3

- 150g dry rice noodles
- 2 tablespoons blanched or red-skin peanuts
- 1 heaped tablespoon smooth Skippy peanut butter
- 2 lemongrass stalks, ends trimmed off and sliced
- 3cm piece fresh galangal, roughly chopped
- 1 tablespoon fish sauce
- Juice of 1 lime
- 1 tablespoon sesame oil
- 1 medium-strength red chilli
- 1 garlic clove
- 200g raw peeled prawns
- 150g minced pork
- 1 tablespoon vegetable oil
- 200g beansprouts
- Handful of coriander, roughly chopped, to garnish

Cook the rice noodles in boiling water according to the pack instructions. Chill the noodles under cool running water, then drain and set aside.

Place the peanuts in a frying pan over a low heat and dry fry them for 5 minutes until slightly charred. Set aside.

Place the peanut butter, lemongrass, galangal, fish sauce, lime juice, sesame oil, red chilli, garlic and 2 tablespoons water in a blender. Pulse until smooth. Coat the prawns and pork in a little of this sauce.

Heat the vegetable oil in a wok and fry the prawns and pork over a moderate heat for 5 minutes until cooked.

Add the beansprouts, noodles, the remaining sauce and continue to cook over a moderate heat, stirring continuously for another few minutes until hot. Spatter with another few drops of fish sauce if you like it tangy.

Finally, garnish with the coriander and peanuts and serve.

PEANUT BUTTER AND CARAMEL ICE CREAM

We've used one form of *dulce de leche*, a heavenly caramel made from condensed milk, in the tiramisu recipe on page 157. Here, the condensed milk is frozen rather than boiled in the tin. We've specified 397g not because this recipe is a precise chemical formula but because that happens to be the weight of the contents of a standard tin.

Serves 4–6

397g tin condensed milk

250ml double cream

100ml full-cream milk

2 tablespoons Skippy peanut butter

Squeezy bottle of caramel sauce or *dulce de leche*

Mix the condensed milk, 200ml of the double cream and the milk thoroughly with a whisk. Freeze until almost solid (this will take approximately 1½ hours).

Mix the peanut butter with the remaining double cream into a thick paste. Stir into the almost-solid ice cream, but not too thoroughly – we want thick blobs to remain.

Squeeze on a good dose of caramel sauce and ripple it through with a shimmy of the hand. Replace in the freezer immediately and leave until fully frozen – about 2½ hours.

Take the ice cream out of the freezer 10 minutes before you need it so that it can soften up.

PEANUT BUTTERCUPS

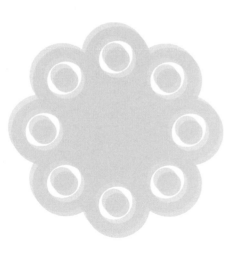

We're rather proud of the name 'peanut buttercups'. Like the flowers, these little cakes are delicate and rather nice. To make them you will need some paper cake cases.

Makes 6–8 cupcakes

For the cakes

100g unsalted butter

2 tablespoons Skippy peanut butter

4 tablespoons maple syrup

1 tablespoon soft light brown sugar

2 medium eggs, beaten

100g self-raising flour

For the icing

1 tablespoon Skippy peanut butter

1 tablespoon maple syrup

1 tablespoon icing sugar

1 tablespoon softened butter

Heat the oven to 180°C/350°F/gas mark 4. Place the paper cake cases on a baking sheet.

Place the butter in a large bowl and heat in the microwave for about 30 seconds or until melted. Add the peanut butter and stir until melted in. Add the maple syrup and brown sugar. Stir until smooth.

Add the the beaten eggs and stir well. Sift in the flour and stir in until smooth. Spoon the mixture into the cake cases.

Bake in the oven for 15 minutes until tinged with a golden lustre. Cool on a wire rack.

While the cakes are cooling, you can make the icing by mixing all the icing ingredients together thoroughly in a small bowl.

When the buttercups are cool, spread the icing over them. Either eat immediately or store in an airtight container. They will keep in a cool place for up to a week.

SKIPPY PEANUT BUTTER AND NUTELLA COOKIES

When you need a quick cookie fix, these are excellent ones to make. They can be mixed and baked within 30 minutes, with a little help from these two marvellous spreads. The only pieces of equipment you need are a bowl, spoon and baking sheet or silicone mat.

Makes 10–12 cookies

125g unsalted butter, at room temperature

125g soft light brown sugar

1 egg, beaten

100g self-raising flour

50g Quaker oats

2 heaped tablespoons Nutella

2 heaped tablespoons Skippy smooth peanut butter

Butter, for greasing

Preheat the oven to 180°C/350°F/gas mark 4. Grease the baking sheet with butter.

Place the butter and sugar in a large bowl and beat them together until pale. Add the egg gradually, beating with the spoon as you go.

Add the flour and the oats and mix well. Finally, add the Nutella and Skippy. Don't mix in the spreads completely; they need to be nice and swirly.

Use a tablespoon to place blobs of cookie mixture on the baking sheet, making sure that they are well spaced as the dough spreads during cooking. Bake for 10–12 minutes until slightly browned.

Let the cookies cool before removing them from the baking sheet, otherwise they will disintegrate. They can be stored in an airtight container for up to a week.

PHILADELPHIA CREAM CHEESE

Cream cheese, that mildly tangy substance you find on bagels and in American-style cheesecakes, is not easy to make. In fact, its existence is down to a happy accident.

William Lawrence, a dairyman from Chester, New York, stumbled upon the formula in 1872 while trying to reproduce a French soft cheese called Neufchâtel. Instead of the expected grainy cheese with a dry rind, he ended up with something velvety, rind-free and delightful. As it was richer and considerably creamier than Neufchâtel, Lawrence decided to call it cream cheese.

A few years later, the Empire Cheese Company of New York started distributing Lawrence's cream cheese in foil wrappers. It was given the name Philadelphia not because it was made there (it wasn't), but because the city in Pennsylvania had a reputation for top-quality produce. In 1903, the business was bought by the Phoenix Cheese Company of New York, which 25 years later merged with the Kraft Cheese Company. This was a good strategic move. The founder of Kraft, James L Kraft, had invented pasteurised cheese back in 1912, and his company's know-how led to a more consistent Philly with an extended shelf life.

Philadelphia quickly became popular outside its native land – in many Latin American countries cream cheese is generically known as *queso filadelfia* –

but it didn't reach the UK until 1960. The first television ads appeared three years later, proclaiming 'At last! Something quite new!', which was true for a country only beginning to emerge from the effects of years of food rationing. It was in 1987, though, that sales really took off, after the nation was treated to the first of a long-running series of ads featuring a ditzy pair of cream cheese-obsessed secretaries. Associating the brand with a couple of airheads initially seemed a strange way to market the product, but the ads were fun and they stuck in the head. They have been replaced by commercials based on the slogan 'A little taste of heaven' but it's still hard to say 'Philadelphia' in anything other than a dizzy blonde voice.

One of the reasons for Philadelphia's success has been the fact that, like Italian mascarpone, it can be used in both savoury and sweet dishes. The greatest episode in its savoury history was surely when an anonymous individual decided to spread some on a bagel and top it with smoked salmon. (To appreciate the genius of this, try eating a similar sandwich without the cream cheese. The words 'tough' and 'chewy' will come to mind).

The eureka moment in the realm of desserts occurred in 1929, when Arnold Reuben, owner of the Turf Restaurant on the corner of 49th Street and Broadway in New York City, decided to make a cheesecake using cream cheese rather than cottage cheese as had hitherto been the norm. The only other ingredients were cream, eggs and sugar, so there was nowhere for the Philly to hide. It came through triumphantly and Reuben's formula for New York cheesecake became standard.

You will find recipes for both main courses and puddings in the pages that follow. Both make use of Philadelphia's creamy texture and its ability to act as a vehicle for other flavours. It is this quality that explains the popularity of versions of the cheese sold premixed with chives or garlic and herbs.

1997 Philadelphia TV Advert.

ROASTED BUTTERNUT SQUASH SOUP WITH PHILADELPHIA

With its sweet orange flesh, the butternut is the king of squashes in our estimation. Here it is elevated into a deliciously velvety realm by the Philadelphia cream cheese. Serve with loads of bread and butter.

Serves 4

1 butternut squash, cut in half lengthways, and seeds scooped out

1 tablespoon butter

1 medium-size onion, roughly diced

1 largish carrot, sliced

2 celery sticks, sliced

200ml tomato passata

2 medium-size potatoes, roughly diced

1 tablespoon Marigold organic vegetable bouillon

½ grated nutmeg

½ teaspoon Maldon sea salt

½ teaspoon freshly ground black pepper

A few sprigs of thyme, chopped

200g Philadelphia cream cheese

Preheat the oven to 200°C/400°F/gas mark 6. Pour 2.5cm water into a roasting tin and place the butternut squash, face down, in the tin. Bake for 35 minutes.

Melt the butter in a large saucepan and add the onion, carrot and celery. Cover and fry gently for 10 minutes, stirring occasionally.

Add 800ml water, the passata and potatoes to the pan. Simmer for 20 minutes, stirring occasionally.

Add the vegetable bouillon, nutmeg, salt, black pepper and thyme. Simmer for 5 minutes.

Stir in the Philadelphia and blend until smooth.

CHORIZO AND SALSA WRAP WITH PHILADELPHIA

The cooling Philadelphia balances the spiciness of the chorizo to great effect in this tasty snack.

Serves 1

75g chorizo, diced (some supermarkets sell it ready-diced)

2 tomatoes, quartered

1 large soft wrap

1 tablespoon Philadelphia cream cheese

½ long, sweet red pepper, cut into strips

Freshly ground black pepper

Gently fry the chorizo in a small frying pan (no oil is needed because so much oozes from the chorizo). Don't fry it too hard because chorizo often seems as though it isn't cooking at all and then goes black.

Once the chorizo is nicely browned, add the tomato and continue to fry for another minute or two.

Spread the wrap with the Philadelphia and then spoon the chorizo and tomato on top in a line. Place the red pepper strips on top of this.

Tightly roll up your wrap. Cut diagonally in the middle. Your wrap is ready to eat.

Filled pasta like ravioli tastes better when freshly made. We'd be lying if we claimed that we regularly make our own, but this dish is an exception. So here is our challenge. Ignore the 'fresh pasta' offered in the supermarket and have a go at making these ravioli yourself. To ensure you get the best possible pasta, it is important to weigh the ingredients accurately. Use flour made from durum wheat (on the packet it will say *semolato di grano duro*) as this is most suitable for the task at hand.

For this recipe you will need a pasta machine and a cutter. We use an 8cm round fluted cutter. Allow 4 ravioli per person for a starter portion and 8 for a main course.

Serves 4 as a starter

For the pasta

250g durum wheat flour

2 large eggs

For the filling

25g basil, leaves removed and finely chopped

100g Philadelphia cream cheese

1 tablespoon tomato purée

2 tablespoons fresh breadcrumbs

1 tablespoon olive oil

Salt and freshly ground black pepper

1 egg, beaten

To serve

Olive oil and Maldon sea salt

Shallow-fried basil leaves (optional)

RAVIOLI WITH BASIL AND PHILADELPHIA

To make the pasta, place the flour in a pile on the worksurface and make a well in the middle for the eggs.

Whisk the eggs gently and pour into the centre of the flour. Using a fork, gradually add more flour from the edges until the egg has become incorporated.

Work with your fingers into a sticky mass and continue until it becomes smooth. It is important that you use up all the flour.

Check to see whether the dough is of the right consistency. Stick your thumb in. If it comes out clean the dough is correct. Knead the dough with the heel of your hand, half turning it, always in the same direction. Knead for at least 5 minutes.

Divide the dough into 3 parts and follow the instructions on your pasta machine to roll it out. You want the dough to be lovely and thin. As the dough becomes ready, lay it down in layers with a sprinkling of flour so it doesn't stick.

To make the filling, combine the basil, Philadelphia, tomato purée, breadcrumbs, olive oil and salt and pepper in a bowl and mix until nice and firm.

Cut out the pasta into 32 rectangles or squares that are bigger than your cutter.

Brush 16 of the squares with the beaten egg wash. Spoon a blob of Philly mixture into the middle of each of these squares.

Press down the remaining 16 squares of pasta on top of the filling, sealing well around the edges and making sure that all the air is pushed out. Then stamp out with the cutter. Your ravioli will look rather pretty.

Bring a large pan of water to the boil. Once it is simmering, add the ravioli one by one and cook for a few minutes. They will rise to the surface. Wait a minute! Now they are ready. Take them out with a slotted spoon.

Serve the ravioli with a dribble of olive oil and a sprinkle of Maldon sea salt, and decorate with crispy basil leaves, if liked.

TOMATO SOUFFLÉ WITH PHILADELPHIA

These soufflés are best cooked when your guests are sitting down. They should be served the instant they come out of the oven.

For this recipe you will need 2 small straight-sided soufflé dishes. Ours are about 4cm high and 8cm across.

Serves 2

50g grated Parmesan cheese

2 large eggs

1 heaped tablespoon Philadelphia cream cheese

1 heaped tablespoon Campbell's condensed cream of tomato soup

1 heaped teaspoon cornflour

Maldon sea salt and freshly ground black pepper

Butter, for greasing

Heat the oven to 180°C/350°F/gas mark 4.

Grease each soufflé dish with butter, then shake a little Parmesan into each one; tap the dishes upside down to remove any excess cheese. The reason we do this is so that the soufflé can rise unimpeded.

Separate the egg yolks and whites and discard (or keep for another time) one of the whites. In a clean dish whisk the egg white until firm.

Combine the egg yolks, Philadelphia, Campbell's soup, cornflour and a little salt and pepper in a bowl and whisk until smooth. Gently fold in the egg white with a spatula. Do this gently so you don't destroy the air bubbles.

Transfer into the soufflé dishes; top with some grated Parmesan. Bake for 12–15 minutes until golden brown on top. Try not to open the oven for the first 10 minutes of cooking; this could result in a collapsed soufflé.

The soufflés should go straight from the oven to the table as they look great for the first few minutes after cooking but gradually deflate after this.

KIDS' BROCCOLI AND MACARONI MELT WITH PHILADELPHIA

Trying to get kids to eat vegetables can be hard work, but even Nick's fussy offspring will wolf this down. For this recipe you will need a large saucepan and a baking dish.

Serves at least 4 kids and 1 adult

1 medium-size head of broccoli, cut into bite-sized florets

200g macaroni

200g Philadelphia cream cheese

2 tablespoons double cream

½ teaspoon Maldon sea salt

100g mature Cheddar cheese, grated

Bring a large saucepan of water to the boil and cook the broccoli for 3–4 minutes. Drain and immediately cool under cold running water.

Preheat the grill to medium.

In the same saucepan, cook the macaroni in boiling water according to the packet instructions. Drain.

Don't cool the macaroni. Replace it immediately in the saucepan after you've drained it and add the Philadelphia, cream, broccoli and salt.

Mix together over a very low heat until the Philadelphia has melted; this won't take more than a minute.

Dollop into the baking dish. Sprinkle the cheese on top and brown under the grill. Your kids will thank you for ever (as if!).

PHILADELPHIA FROZEN CHEESECAKE

Keep the recipe for this cheesecake base a secret or every Tom, Dick and Harry will be copying it. You will need a baking tray of about 30 x 20cm with sides at least 5cm deep.

Serves 6–8

The base

    50g almonds

    50g blanched hazelnuts

    200g ginger biscuits

    150g butter, melted, plus extra for greasing

    100g soft light brown sugar

The topping

    300ml double cream

    3 tablespoons clear honey

    397g tin condensed milk

    400g Philadelphia cream cheese

Preheat the oven to 180°C/350°F/gas mark 4. Grease the baking tin and then line with greaseproof paper.

To make the base, bake the almonds and hazelnuts in the oven for 8 minutes. Allow the nuts to cool, then place them in a food processor and blend until coarse. Remove from the processor and set aside.

Reduce the oven temperature to 160°C/325°F/gas mark 3.

Place the ginger biscuits in the processor and blend them until coarse.

Combine the blended nuts and biscuits with the melted butter and brown sugar in a bowl. Spoon onto the prepared baking tray and flatten evenly with a spatula or palette knife.

Bake in the oven for 15 minutes. Leave to cool.

Pour the cream and honey into a large bowl. Whisk until the cream has thickened but is still runny. Add the Philadelphia and condensed milk. Whisk until smooth.

Spoon this mixture onto the base and level it off with a palette knife. Freeze the cheesecake until solid.

Once frozen, allow the cheesecake to defrost for a few minutes, just long enough to remove it from the tray and cut it into portions. The cheesecake can either be eaten immediately or portions stored in an airtight container in the freezer for up to a couple of months.

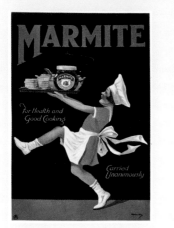

MARMITE

Marmite, to cut a long story short, is a pungent paste made from dead yeast cells.

For centuries, brewers simply threw away the yeast they had used to make beer once it had done its primary work. Then, in 1680, the Dutch scientist Anton van Leewenhoek shoved a sample of yeast under a microscope and saw that it was made up of cells. The stuff was alive! Louis Pasteur later discovered that it was made up of tiny plants, and in the 19th century a German chemist called Justus Liebig established that spent brewer's yeast could be made into an edible paste. All that remained was for somebody to work out how to tap this abundant resource efficiently.

The answer was provided in 1902 by a firm based in Burton-on-Trent in the English Midlands, home of the giant Bass brewery. The precise manufacturing process was kept secret, but essentially it involved killing off the yeast cells and straining off their thick cell walls. Then various vegetable and spice extracts were added to round off the flavour. The result was a thick, nutritious paste that the author Bill Bryson has described as 'an edible yeast extract with the visual properties of an industrial lubricant'. The makers called it Marmite after a French type of earthenware cooking pot. It was very salty and packed with glutamines that gave it a powerful savoury taste.

After the discovery of vitamins in 1912, it was shown that brewer's yeast was one of the richest sources of B vitamins in existence. The Marmite Food Company consequently based its advertisements on the slogan 'Marmite is good for you'. And it is. It contains almost no fat or sugar and babies love to be weaned on it, (except those who don't!). The manufacturers have long recognised that you either love the stuff or you hate it. In fact, they have embraced this truth to the extent that visitors to their website are presented on arrival with a choice of Marmite bottles to click on: a 'love' version with angels' wings plus halo and a 'hate' jar with bats' wings and red horns.

Marmite vs Vegemite

Let's not beat about the bush here. Marmite and Vegemite are extremely divisive foods. They are too strongly and distinctively flavoured to be neutral about. Some people (Johnny) absolutely detest them. Others (Nick) would eat them on their death beds. Fortunately for the manufacturers, there are more than enough people in the second category. At least half the population will relish the recipes that follow.

The two brands may look similar to the non-connoisseur but there are important differences between them. Indeed, fans of either are likely to go apoplectic if you equate it with the other one. Australians in particular regard the distinctiveness of Vegemite as an issue of national honour. In the interests of both accuracy and Anglo-Aussie harmony, we have therefore decided to give each product its own chapter. Both have a tangy flavour somewhat reminiscent of soy sauce but with a pronounced twist.

MARMITE, ONION AND ROASTED TOMATO TART

This tart looks as good as it tastes. You'll need a 25–28cm, non-stick shallow pizza pan to cook it in.

Serves 4 as a starter or 2 as a main course

> **20–25 baby onions, halved, or 2 medium-size onions, roughly chopped**
>
> **300g cherry tomatoes**
>
> **1 tablespoon olive oil**
>
> **1 tablespoon balsamic vinegar**
>
> **1 teaspoon dried mixed herbs**
>
> **375g pack ready-rolled puff pastry**
>
> **125g mozzarella cheese**
>
> **Good squirt of Marmite (best from a squeezy pot)**
>
> **Salt and freshly ground black pepper**

Preheat the oven to 120°C/250°F/gas mark ½.

Place the onions and tomatoes on a baking tray. Pour over the olive oil and balsamic vinegar and scatter on the mixed herbs. Season well and toss the ingredients around until everything is coated with the yummy stuff. Roast for 1 hour.

Increase the oven temperature to 220°C/425°F/gas mark 7.

Unroll your puff pastry until it is flat on the worksurface. Turn the pizza dish face down on the pastry and cut around it. If the pastry isn't quite big enough sprinkle a little flour on top and roll out a little further with a rolling pin. Gather up the pastry and press firmly into the pizza tin.

Thinly slice the mozzarella and lay it evenly onto the puff pastry. Top with the tomatoes and onions and all the lovely juices. You can squish down the tomatoes if you like. Watch out they don't squirt over you.

Take the squeezy Marmite and leave a good old trail either in a zig-zag motion or spiral all over the tart.

Bake for 15–20 minutes until the pastry has puffed up nicely and is golden brown.

One of the culinary wonders of the modern world is ready-rolled puff pastry. Nick remembers the pain of making it at college. The *umami*-rich flavour (see page 124) of Marmite lends itself to meatloaf.

MEATLOAF ROLL WITH MARMITE

Serves 4

375g ready-rolled puff pastry (40 x 24cm is the ideal size for this recipe)

1 tablespoon Marmite

1 tablespoon butter

500g minced beef

1 medium-size onion, finely chopped

2 garlic cloves, finely chopped

1 tablespoon mixed herbs (we use *herbes de Provence*)

2 teaspoons paprika

Handful of flat-leaf parsley, roughly chopped

1 teaspoon Maldon sea salt

Freshly ground black pepper

1 egg, beaten

Preheat the oven to 160°C/325°F/ gas mark 3.

Unroll the pastry and place it on to a worksurface with one of the longer sides facing you. Mix the Marmite and butter together in a small bowl. Spread all over the pastry.

In a large bowl, mix together the beef, onion, garlic, mixed herbs, paprika, parsley, salt and pepper. It is easiest to do this with your bare hands. Squeeze this mixture into a long sausage alongside the rolled out pastry. It should be a little shorter than the pastry (approximately 36cm).

Transfer the sausage on to the pastry, leaving a gap at each end. Lift up the edge of the pastry closest to you and slowly roll it up around the meat like a giant sausage roll.

Transfer the roll to a baking sheet. Squeeze in the ends and brush the top with egg (this makes the pastry nice and shiny).

Bake for 35–40 minutes. Slice to serve.

VEGEMITE

I said, 'Do you speak-ah my language?'
He just smiled and gave me a Vegemite sandwich.

So sang the Australian band Men at Work in their global 1982 hit *Down Under.* The man who dispenses the said snack to the hero of the song is actually a muscular six-foot four-inch Belgian, but the point is that it would be hard to imagine a more eloquent way of showing an Aussie that you're on his wavelength than giving him a Vegemite sandwich.

The phrase 'happy little Vegemite(s)', originally used in an advertising jingle in the 1950s, has become an essential part of the Australian lexicon. It means roughly the same as 'happy bunny' everywhere else.

The flavour of Vegemite is not as intense as Marmite, although that description admittedly leaves plenty of room for intensity. If you're in doubt about which you prefer we'd advise you to acquire a jar of each.

VEGEMITE
KRAFT
CONCENTRATED YEAST EXTRACT

THE SPREAD AUSTRALIANS GROW UP ON.

Press advertisement, 1988. The film *Crocodile Dundee* probably influenced the idea behind this campaign.

BUTTER VEGEMITE CROISSANTS

****

These savoury croissants represent an unexpected fusion between Australian and French cuisine. They are made with ready-to-bake croissant dough. The brand we use is Sara Lee, but there are others.

Serves 4

240g tin ready-to-bake croissant mix

2 teaspoons Vegemite

4 teaspoons butter, at room temperature

Preheat the oven to 180°C/350°F/ gas mark 4.

It's funny old stuff, ready-to-use croissant dough. First you must carefully remove it from its tin and unfurl it into a roll. The next thing you do is tear, or preferably cut, along the dotted line to reveal 4 triangles of dough with 2 long sides and a short side.

Place half a teaspoon of Vegemite at the short end of the dough along with 1 teaspoon of butter. Gently roll up each croissant, place on a baking sheet and bake for 15–18 minutes, until golden brown.

VEGEMITE AND CARAWAY CHEESE SWIRLS

These swirls are thin, savoury biscuits. They look so good you could even package them up as a present.

Makes 24 biscuits

> Flour, for dusting
> 250g ready-made shortcrust pastry
> 2 teaspoons Vegemite
> 2 teaspoons butter, softened
> 100g mature Cheddar cheese, grated
> 2 teaspoons caraway seeds
> Butter, for greasing

Dust a worksurface with flour and roll out the pastry into a square approximately 30 x 30cm, as thin as you can get it without it breaking. Turn the pastry occasionally and keep sprinkling the surface with flour to prevent the pastry from sticking.

Mix the Vegemite and butter together in a small bowl and spread it evenly over the pastry.

Sprinkle the grated cheese evenly over the pastry. Sprinkle the caraway seeds evenly on top of the cheese.

Roll the pastry up tightly from one side to form a long roll. Chill the roll in the fridge for 30 minutes.

Preheat the oven to 160°C/325°F/gas mark 3. Grease a baking tray.

Take the pastry out of the fridge and, with a sharp knife, cut it into 5mm sections. Don't worry if the pastry mis-shapes a bit when you cut it; it will still taste delicious.

Lay the slices onto the greased baking tray and bake for 15–20 minutes, or until the pastry is crispy and slightly coloured.

Remove from the oven and transfer the swirls to a cooling rack. Once cool, store in an airtight container for up to 1 week.

HEINZ TOMATO KETCHUP

When we were growing up in the 1970s, some of our friends' parents displayed an irrational snobbery about Heinz tomato ketchup.

It was probably rooted in the not entirely unfounded suspicion that were it to be allowed on the table, we kids would plaster it on every foodstuff placed in front of us. But would this really have been so odd? After all, in many Asian countries everything is doused in soy sauce and residents of the Yucatán can't taste anything unless it's been liberally sprinkled with fiery habañero chilli. To have a basic sauce is an anthropological constant. Such condiments improve palatability and aid digestion. And if the Earth has a basic sauce, it's surely Heinz tomato ketchup. The sauce is sold in containers ranging from bottles and catering packs to sachets, and if you are the average citizen of the word (citizen, not household), you get through a shade under two of them every year. Yes, that's right, annual production of the thick red sauce hovers around the eleven billion unit mark.

The story of how the sauce came to occupy this exalted position begins with its creator making a revolutionary decision. When 16-year-old Henry Heinz (born 1844) decided to start selling the horseradish sauce he had taken to making at his home in Sharpsburgh, Pennsylvania, he elected to package it in clear bottles. That way, customers could see for themselves that the sauce was not adulterated with turnip or anything worse. In an era in which unscrupulous manufacturers were not beyond bulking up their products with woodchips, this pioneering move proved immensely popular. When Heinz founded the company that bears his name in 1869, he committed to a policy of avoiding the use of artificial additives or preservatives.

In 1876, the firm unveiled what would become its definitive product: Heinz tomato ketchup. The word ketchup is thought to derive from the Chinese *ke tsiap*, meaning 'brine of pickled fish'. By the time 17th century British and Dutch traders came across the term in South East Asia, its usage had been extended to cover sauces based on the brine used to pickle pretty much anything. The sharp taste of such condiments went down well with European travellers, and when they returned home they brought recipes for *ke tsiap* with them.

In due course, a liking for the sauce spread to America. In the early days, however, people couldn't agree on a name for it. In 1831, the author of *The Domestic Chemist* (a popular science book) defined ketchup as 'a sauce of which the name can be pronounced by everybody but spelled by nobody'. There was a similar lack of unanimity about what ketchup/catchup/katsup should be made from. Versions based on mushrooms, walnuts and seafood were all popular. Recipes involving tomatoes, or 'love apples' as they were then known, didn't appear until the early 19th century.

The first commercial tomato ketchups were made with what were euphemistically called 'trimmings' from the canning industry, in other words bruised, rotten or otherwise substandard fruit. Henry Heinz's sauce was different. It was made with good, ripe tomatoes and plenty of them. It takes 132 grams of tomatoes to make 100 grams of Heinz ketchup (the difference in weight is accounted for by evaporation), hence its celebrated thickness. This is something the manufacturers take very seriously. Any batch that pours unaided faster than 0.028mph is rejected.

What more can we say about this great sauce? It is perfectly balanced, sweet but not too sweet, vinegary but not too vinegary and has just the right level of spice. It contains a useful antioxidant called lycopene but no GM ingredients or other junk. And as we mean to show you, it is a fine and versatile cooking ingredient.

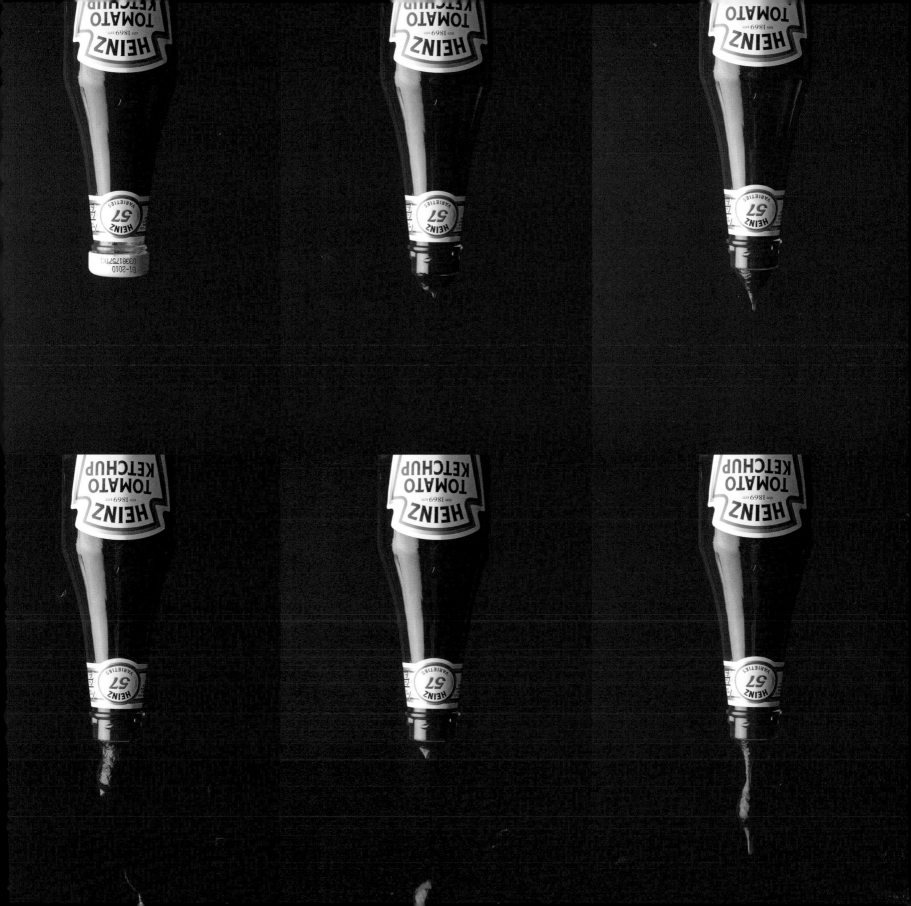

STICKY KETCHUP SAUSAGES IN A BAGUETTE

OK, this is a glorified hot dog, but the accent should be firmly on the 'glorified'.

Serves 3

2 heaped teaspoons dried oregano

1½ teaspoons mustard powder

1 tablespoon clear honey

1 tablespoon wholegrain mustard

1 tablespoon Heinz tomato ketchup, plus extra to serve

6 pork sausages

Salt and freshly ground black pepper

1 baguette

Preheat the oven to 150°C/300°F/gas mark 2.

Mix together the oregano, mustard powder, honey, mustard, ketchup and seasoning.

Place the sausages in a baking tin and spoon the ketchup mixture evenly on top.

Bake in the oven for 25 minutes. Increase the temperature to 180°C/350°F/gas mark 4 for the last 5 minutes and pop the baguette in at the same time (no longer or the sausages will burn).

Cut the baguette in half lengthways. Throw the sausages in, plus any leftover sauce from the bottom of the pan. Squirt liberally with tomato ketchup. Heaven!

SEARED SEAFOOD WITH MARIE ROSE DRESSING

One of our favourite ways to use Heinz tomato ketchup is to make a Marie Rose or Thousand Island dressing. Everyone knows the importance of this sauce to a classic prawn cocktail. This recipe shows it goes pretty well with squid and monkfish, too.

Serves 1

16 raw tiger prawns, tail shells left on

200g monkfish fillets, cut into chunks

2 medium-size squid tubes, cleaned and cut into 8 pieces

Juice of 1 lemon

2 garlic cloves, finely chopped

Few sprigs of thyme, finely chopped

Salt and freshly ground black pepper

1 tablespoon Heinz tomato ketchup

1 tablespoon Hellmann's mayonnaise

Handful of rocket

Splash of olive oil

Lay out the prawns, monkfish and squid in a bowl. Squeeze over the lemon juice, add the garlic and thyme and season well.

Combine the ketchup and mayonnaise to make the Marie Rose dressing, and set aside.

Heat the olive oil in a large non-stick pan until it is starting to smoke.

Fry the seafood in batches, one sort at a time, over a moderate to high heat (watch out for the squid, it spits). The squid needs cooking for a minute on each side, no longer or it will toughen; the prawns for 4 minutes, and the monkfish perhaps for a shade longer depending on the size of the pieces.

Serve the seafood with the rocket and a liberal dollop of Marie Rose.

CHILLI PRAWNS
WITH TOMATO KETCHUP

This is another dish that demonstrates the affinity between the prawn and Heinz tomato ketchup. The affinity between Johnny and fresh coriander is considerably weaker. He thinks it tastes of soap, but he knows he's in a minority and Nick overruled him in this recipe.

Serves 2

200g raw peeled tiger prawns

1 tablespoon Heinz tomato ketchup

2 teaspoons fish sauce

Small handful of coriander, roughly chopped

½ red chilli, chopped

1 tablespoon chopped fresh root ginger

1 garlic clove, chopped

1 tablespoon vegetable oil

In a small bowl, coat the prawns with the ketchup, fish sauce, coriander, chilli, ginger and garlic.

Heat the oil in a large non-stick frying pan or wok until it is shimmering. Fry the prawns over a moderate heat for 2–3 minutes on each side.

Serve immediately, with the sauce from the pan.

BAKED TORTILLA WRAP WITH SPICY CHICKEN AND KETCHUP

✳✳✳✳✳✳✳✳✳✳✳✳✳✳✳✳✳✳✳✳✳✳✳✳✳✳✳✳✳✳✳✳✳✳✳✳✳

This feisty wrap takes less than 20 minutes to prepare, and makes a satisfying lunch or light tea.

Serves 1

2 slices pre-sliced Jarlsberg, Leerdammer or Emmenthal cheese

1 fresh tortilla wrap (20–24cm)

½ cooked chicken breast or 1 cooked chicken drumstick, meat removed and sliced

4 cherry tomatoes, halved

Squirt of Heinz tomato ketchup

Few drops of Tabasco pepper sauce, optional

2 red pepper rings

Sprinkle of dried oregano

Salt and freshly ground black pepper

Preheat the oven to 180°C/350°F/ gas mark 4.

Place the 2 slices of cheese side by side in the middle of the wrap. Lay the slices of chicken in a line on top of the cheese, followed by the cherry tomatoes.

Top with a good squirt of tomato ketchup, and, if you like spicy food, a few drops of Tabasco.

Pinch the red pepper rings and open them straight. Lay them on top of the ketchup. Finally, season with the oregano, salt and pepper.

Roll the wrap tightly closed, place on a baking tray and bake for 10 minutes.

Leave for a couple of minutes before you eat because those tomatoes can be very hot!

PORK TENDERLOIN WITH SWEET AND SOUR SAUCE

Nick's oriental fare has come on in leaps and bounds since he married a Chinese lady. This tangy dish is one of the fruits of their nuptials. The quantities specified in this recipe produce quite a sour sweet-and-sour sauce. If you prefer it sweeter, just add another tablespoon of sugar. The ketchup acts as a natural thickener and gives the sauce a lovely lustre.

Serves 2–3

300g pork tenderloin, sliced

2 teaspoons fish sauce

1 tablespoon sesame oil

2.5cm piece fresh root ginger, very thinly sliced

2 garlic cloves, chopped

3 spring onions, chopped

½ chicken stock cube

1 tablespoon Kikkoman soy sauce

3 tablespoons vinegar (we used rice vinegar, but cider vinegar or white wine vinegar are fine)

3 tablespoons Heinz tomato ketchup

1 tablespoon sugar

Juice of ½ lime

Combine the pork tenderloin with the fish sauce.

Heat the sesame oil in a wok and fry the pork for 3 minutes on each side over a moderate to high heat, until nicely browned. Turn the heat right down.

Add the ginger, garlic and spring onions, and gently fry for a couple of minutes. Add the stock cube, soy sauce, vinegar, ketchup, sugar and lime juice, along with 4 tablespoons water.

Gently heat. Simmer for a few minutes and the dish is ready to serve.

COLMAN'S MUSTARD

There is no shortage of mustard in the world. It can be grainy or smooth, vinegared or unvinegared, plain or flavoured, and can lie anywhere on the heat spectrum from mild to demonic.

Some like it grey and French, others prefer it brown and German. In our opinion, however, nothing beats the pungent taste of vivid yellow English mustard, the definitive version of which has been manufactured by Colman's of Norwich for almost 200 years.

The key ingredients in Colman's mustard are ground white and brown mustard seeds. The former provide the sensation in the nose that makes you want to sneeze if you overindulge, the latter are responsible for the (considerable) heat on the tongue. Together they pack quite a punch. Other mustards seem puny in comparison.

Jeremiah Colman, the founder of the brand, hailed from Norfolk in East Anglia. He began his career as a regular flour miller but, in 1814, he acquired premises a few miles south of the city of Norwich that presented him with three alternatives. He could use the mill to produce wheat flour, he could make mustard like the previous owner, or he could manufacture paper there like one of his predecessors. Fortunately for lovers of hot dogs, roast beef and ham sandwiches, he chose to concentrate on mustard.

Colman ran the business as a family concern and after nine years went into partnership with his adopted nephew James, who was still on the shop floor mixing mustard flours by hand 20 years later. The firm went from strength to strength but it was James' son Jeremiah James who proved the real pioneer. He was a shrewd businessman with a powerful social conscience. He instituted revolutionary welfare measures such as the opening of a school for the workers' children and the employment of the nation's first industrial nurse. He also introduced the company's famous bull's head logo in 1855. It was initially designed to denote one of the firm's other products, namely laundry starch, but Colman's soon spotted that it perfectly conveyed the chief characteristic of the mustard: strength.

Colman's mustard is an incredibly useful substance to have about the house. It has culinary applications in dishes as diverse as salad dressings and piccalilli, and though we haven't actually tested this theory, an internet character called Mustard James claims that half a teaspoon of the mustard improves the chocolate sauce used for profiteroles. The utility of the hot yellow sauce doesn't end with food, however. If you have a cold or a sore throat, instead of reaching for the medicine cabinet try imitating your great-great grandmother by applying a mustard plaster. Just smear some Colman's on a wash flannel and place it on the back of your neck for a quarter of an hour (but remove it if you feel a burning sensation!). That should drive out most bugs. The mustard also apparently does a great job as a fertiliser for daffodils, making them yellower. You can even use it as an emergency adhesive for dislodged tiles.

There's a lot to be said for buying Colman's mustard in powdered form. It keeps for longer that way and you can mix it to whatever strength you like. But as we're working on the assumption that you want to do as little work as possible, the recipes that follow are based on Colman's in its 'wet' premixed form. If you do choose to use the dry stuff, just make up the amounts specified.

CHEDDAR AND MUSTARD
BISCUITS

These little biscuits are perfect with a slab of cheese or on their own as a savoury snack.

Makes about 20 biscuits

- 75g mature Cheddar cheese
- 2 teaspoons Colman's mustard
- 150g plain flour
- 100g butter, at room temperature
- ½ teaspoon Maldon sea salt
- ½ teaspoon freshly ground black pepper

Place all the ingredients in the food processor and pulse until they start to form a ball.

Turn the dough onto a worksurface and roll into a sausage about 4cm in diameter. Cover in clingfilm and chill in the fridge for half an hour or so.

Preheat the oven to 180°C/350°F/gas mark 4. Grease a baking tray.

Slice the rolls into 1cm-thick discs and place on the baking tray. Bake the biscuits for 18–20 minutes, checking them towards the end to make sure they aren't burning (as all ovens vary in temperature).

Allow to cool and then enjoy! They will keep in an airtight container for up to 2 weeks.

Point of sale card that would have been used as a shop display.

ENGLISH MUFFINS WITH MUSTARD AND CHEDDAR

You can't beat a good English muffin. Here's how to make them from scratch.

This is one of the easiest of risen breads to make. Muffins are small and manageable, you don't need any specialised equipment, and they freeze really well. Kids love them.

You will need an 8cm round cutter and either a large heavy-based frying pan or a flat griddle (if you are lucky enough to possess one).

Makes 12 muffins

> 500g unbleached white bread flour
>
> 2 teaspoons Maldon sea salt (they really need this much, believe us)
>
> 15g fresh yeast (this freezes well so don't worry if you've bought too much)
>
> 75g mature Cheddar cheese, finely grated
>
> 400ml lukewarm milk
>
> 2 teaspoons Colman's mustard
>
> Flour, for dusting
>
> Semolina or rice flour, also for dusting

Mix together the flour and salt in a large bowl.

Take the fresh yeast and grated Cheddar. Rub them together with your fingers to make a paste.

Pour in a little of the milk and add the mustard. Cream the mixture and keep adding milk until it's all gone in.

Add to the flour and give it a good old stir. The mixture will become firm and elastic after a minute or two.

Scrape the sides of the bowl down with a plastic scraper and turn out onto a floured surface. Knead for a couple of minutes, sprinkling on a little extra flour if it is sticking to your fingers.

Return the dough to the bowl. Lay a damp tea towel on top and leave to rise in a warm place for 45 minutes to 1 hour, or until the dough has approximately doubled in size.

Scrape the dough out in one piece onto a lightly floured surface and throw a little flour on the surface of the dough.

Knock back. This is essentially deflating some of the large bubbles that have been formed by the yeast. Do this by pressing down firmly with the heel of your hand in several places.

Press out with the heel of your hand to approximately 1.5–2cm thick. Cut out as many muffins as possible with the cutter. You should get 12–14.

Sprinkle a flat tray with semolina and carefully place the muffins on it. Leave to rise for 20–30 minutes in a warm (ideally humid) place.

Place the pan or griddle onto a low to moderate heat and dry fry the muffins until nicely toasted on each side, approximately 5–7 minutes. Our pan is 26cm, which accommodates 6 muffins, so we can cook them in two batches.

An alternative is to let the muffins rise slowly in the fridge overnight and fry them in the morning.

These muffins freeze very well but don't forget to cut them along the middle before you do – so that you can pop them straight into the toaster while still frozen.

SEA BASS GRAVADLAX, MUSTARD AND DILL SAUCE

Lax actually means 'salmon' in Swedish. That's what gravadlax is usually made with, but for this one we've used the equally good sea bass. Technically, therefore, it should be called 'gravad-Swedish word for sea bass', but since we don't know what that is we've stretched the original term.

The key to getting this recipe right lies in the fish. It must be fresh. When buying sea bass, look for a glistening, firm fish with clear, bulging eyes. It should smell, well, not too fishy. The perfect fish for this recipe should weigh just under a kilo, from which you need two well-scaled, boneless fillets. Get the fishmonger to do this. Tell him to be thorough!

Now you are in possession of your sea bass fillets, check them for bones, especially the lateral ones that poke out when you run your finger down the centre of the fish (the pinbones). They should come out with the help of a pair of tweezers.

This fish needs a 24-hour cure in the fridge before it is ready.

Serves 4

For the fish

    2 sea bass fillets, clean and dry

    Maldon sea salt

    Brown sugar

    Zest of 1 lemon

    Handful of roughly chopped dill

For the sauce

    2 teaspoons Colman's mustard

    1 tablespoon Hellmann's mayonnaise

    A little dill, finely chopped

Lay the sea bass fillets skin side down on a plate.

Sprinkle the fillets with sea salt. How much? Well, never so much that there is more than one crystal on top of another. Do the same with the brown sugar. A little less sugar than salt please.

Finish off with the lemon zest and dill. Cover with clingfilm and leave in the fridge for 24 hours.

For the sauce, simply combine all three ingredients in a bowl.

After 24 hours, wipe all the excess curing ingredients off the fish. Lay the fish on a chopping board, skin side down. The tail should be furthest away from you.

Slice the fish away from you starting with the tail end; as thin as possible. Ideally, you want to leave the skin behind after you have sliced the whole fish (but don't worry; the fish will taste nice even if you hack it to pieces). Take your time. You can do this in advance.

Serve the sliced fish with the sauce.

FRIED PORK WONTONS WITH MUSTARD

Wonton pastry is very thin and cut into small squares. It is available from Asian supermarkets in packets of 50 leaves or so, and is pleasingly inexpensive.

Wontons are little parcels, traditionally stuffed with pork and shrimps, that are either boiled in soup or deep fried. We are going to fry ours.

Makes 20–24 wontons

For the wontons

> 200g minced pork
>
> 2 teaspoons Colman's mustard
>
> 1 tablespoon crème fraîche
>
> 2 spring onions, thinly sliced
>
> ¼ teaspoon Maldon sea salt
>
> Freshly ground black pepper
>
> 1 egg, beaten
>
> Vegetable oil, for shallow frying

For the dip

> 2 tablespoons Hellmann's mayonnaise
>
> 2 teaspoons Colman's mustard

To make the dip, simply combine the mayo with the mustard in a small bowl.

To make the wontons, combine the pork with the mustard, crème fraîche, spring onions and salt. Season with pepper and stir until well combined.

Place a wonton wrapper on a worksurface and brush with the beaten egg. Using a teaspoon, place a blob of the pork mixture in the middle of the wrapper. Fold over and press down firmly. Repeat to make 20–24 wontons, or until you have used all the filling.

Heat the vegetable oil in a wok or frying pan and shallow-fry the wontons in batches over a moderate heat (180°C) for approximately 2½ minutes on each side. Keep the fried wontons warm and repeat until they are all cooked.

Serve immediately with the dip.

HOT SALT BEEF WRAP WITH COLMAN'S MUSTARD

Get some soft tortilla wraps from the supermarket and indulge yourself. These perky tubes of flavour can be rolled in advance and then just take 15 minutes to bake in the oven. The sauerkraut provides both crunch and a vinegary tang.

You will need a 40cm square of greaseproof paper.

Serves 1

3 slices Jarlsberg cheese
1 large soft tortilla wrap
4–6 thin slices salt beef or pastrami
2 tablespoons sauerkraut
50g tube Colman's mustard (you aren't going to use all of it, it's just easier to squirt)
Freshly ground black pepper

Preheat the oven to 200°C/400°F/ gas mark 6.

Place the slices of Jarlsberg next to each other along the middle of the wrap. Lay the slices of meat in a line on top.

Put the sauerkraut in a sieve over a bowl and press down with a spoon to remove any excess liquid. Place the sauerkraut on top of the beef and spread it out in a line.

Squeeze some Colman's mustard on top of the sauerkraut. This will make it pretty hot, so you know what to do if you want less heat. Season with pepper.

Roll the wrap up tightly. Lay it on the greaseproof square, and then wrap the paper around it.

Bake in the oven for 15 minutes. Unwrap and enjoy.

STILTON AND MUSTARD SOUP

This is the kind of soup you can imagine Victorian gents tucking into. The hotness of the mustard complements the creaminess of the Stilton nicely. Serve with lots of crusty bread.

Serves 4

- 20g unsalted butter
- 3 celery sticks, roughly sliced
- 1 large onion, roughly chopped
- 2 medium-size potatoes, roughly diced
- 150g Stilton cheese, roughly chopped
- 1 tablespoon Colman's mustard
- ½ teaspoon Maldon sea salt
- 1 tablespoon Marigold organic vegetable bouillon
- 6 fresh sage leaves
- Sprig or two of thyme
- 1 heaped tablespoon crème fraîche

Melt the butter in a large saucepan, add the celery and onion, cover and cook over a gentle heat until soft. This should take about 10 minutes.

Add 800ml water and the potatoes to the pan. Simmer for 20–25 minutes until the potatoes are soft.

Add the Stilton, mustard, salt, vegetable bouillon, sage and thyme to the pan. Simmer for a couple of minutes until the Stilton has melted and then blend, using a hand blender, until smooth.

Stir in the crème fraîche and the soup is ready.

HELLMANN'S MAYONNAISE

There are various explanations as to the origin of mayonnaise, that creamy emulsion of oil, vinegar and egg yolk that appears in millions of sandwiches on a daily basis.

Some claim that the sauce was born in the French city of Bayonne and was originally known as 'Bayonnaise', but that at some stage the 'b' got lost and replaced with an 'm'. Others hold that the name 'mayonnaise' is a derivative of the French verb *magner*, which means to stir or make by hand. Still others say that it was named in honour of the Duc de Mayenne, who famously insisted on finishing his meal of chicken with cold sauce before commencing the Battle of Arques in 1589. (In some ways, this made him a French version of Sir Francis Drake, who had displayed a similarly unhurried attitude to a game of bowls the previous year, despite the rapid approach of the Spanish Armada. The key difference was that Drake won his battle whereas de Mayenne was defeated.)

The most popular theory, however, is that mayonnaise was created in 1756, after French forces led by the Duc de Richelieu ousted the British from Mahon, the capital of the Mediterranean island of Minorca. The menu for the subsequent victory banquet called for a sauce made from cream and eggs. Unfortunately, the Duc's chef couldn't get hold of any cream, so he substituted olive oil. The resulting sauce, which he named after the city of Mahon, was a terrific hit.

The riddle of the historical origin of mayonnaise may never be solved, but there is no such doubt about the provenance of the world's number one brand. The recipe was devised by Nina, the wife of a German immigrant to the US called Richard Hellmann. In 1905, the couple opened a delicatessen in New York, with Frau Hellmann's mayo playing a starring role in the store's salads. The sauce proved so popular that the Hellmanns started selling it in wooden 'butter boats', before moving on to glass jars. They initially sold two versions of the recipe. The premium variety, which was adorned with a blue ribbon, fairly flew off the shelves. In 1912, to make life simpler, Hellmann designed a label featuring the ribbon motif to replace the actual strips of fabric. The blue ribbon logo remains on jars of Hellmann's to this day.

There is, of course, a lot to be said for homemade mayonnaise, but preparing it is both laborious and tricky. The first stage is relatively easy – you just beat egg yolks together with vinegar or lemon juice plus seasonings – but then things get more complicated. You have to add olive or vegetable oil in various stages and one drop at a time, beating the mixture furiously all the while.

Any miscalculations will leave you with a right old mess. Even if you are successful, your mayonnaise will only keep for a week. Under most circumstances it is therefore much better to let Hellmann's take the strain. After all, the company has had more than a century to perfect the art.

Hellmann's mayonnaise is wonderfully smooth and creamy. You could even call it fluffy. It is also a great deal more versatile than its standard use as a lubricant for sandwiches might suggest. Recently, for example, it has become a commonplace sushi ingredient, as in the popular California roll. In this chapter you will find some fine Hellmann's-based recipes, plus instructions for transforming the basic mayo into a handful of other delectable sauces.

SIBERIAN POTATO SALAD WITH HELLMANN'S MAYONNAISE

Veronica, Nick's 18-year-old kick-boxing, karate black belt lodger from Novosibirsk, made him this salad after he implied that Siberia didn't have much of a culinary heritage. She certainly proved him wrong as it's delicious. particularly when served with smoked fish and caviar with a hunk of rye bread and butter.

Serves 4

- 2 medium-size potatoes, cut into 1cm cubes
- 2 medium-size carrots, cut into 1cm cubes
- 4 large eggs
- 6 medium-size gherkins, cut into 1cm cubes
- Sprig of flat-leaf parsley, roughly chopped
- 2 spring onions, roughly chopped
- Sprig of dill, roughly chopped (optional)
- 3 tablespoons Hellmann's mayonnaise
- Juice of ½ lemon
- Salt and freshly ground black pepper

Bring a large pan of water to the boil. Add the potato and carrot cubes to the pan and boil for 2 minutes. Add the eggs to the pan and boil for a further 8 minutes.

Remove the eggs from the pan and cool under running water. Drain the vegetables and cool in the same way. Peel and chop the eggs into 1cm pieces.

Mix the vegetables, eggs, gherkins, parsley, spring onions and dill together in a large serving bowl, but be gentle; if you overmix the salad it can look mushy.

Put the mayonnaise in a small bowl and add the lemon juice. Stir well, then gently fold into the main mixture. Season with salt and pepper.

FISH FINGERS COATED WITH OATS AND CORNFLAKES WITH HELLMANN'S TARTAR SAUCE

This recipe uses no fewer than four of the brands featured in this book. When we say 'Hellmann's tartar sauce' what we really mean is tartar sauce made with Hellmann's mayonnaise.

It's fun to make your own fish fingers. Make sure you get your fish from a sustainable source (check with your fishmonger if you're not sure). And of course, the best accompaniment is loads of chips.

Serves 2

For the fish fingers

200g haddock fillet, cut into strips

Small pile of flour

1 egg, beaten

80g Quaker oats

50g Kellogg's cornflakes, crunched up in your hand

Oil, for deep frying

For the tartar sauce

2 tablespoons Hellmann's mayonnaise

1 tablespoon chopped dill

Juice of ½ lemon

½ teaspoon Colman's mustard

1 teaspoon capers, chopped

1 medium-size gherkin, finely chopped

Freshly ground black pepper

First, make the sauce: simply place all the ingredients in a bowl and mix well.

To make the fish fingers, lightly coat the haddock strips in the flour. Make sure that when you do this the fillets are not too wet. Pat them dry with kitchen paper first if necessary.

Combine the oats and crunched-up cornflakes in a shallow bowl. Dip a strip of fish in the egg so that it is coated, then dip it into the oat and cornflake mixture and roll it around until it is covered. Repeat with the rest of the fish strips.

Deep-fry the fish fingers in moderately hot oil (180°C/350°F) for 5–6 minutes, or until golden brown. Don't crowd the pan – cook in batches if necessary.

Serve the fish with the tartar sauce.

STIR-FRIED PORK WITH HELLMANN'S MAYONNAISE AND OYSTER SAUCE

We love this dish. Why? It is creamy, sophisticated, aromatic, moreish and blatantly indulgent – yet it takes a maximum of 15 minutes to prepare and cook.

Make sure all the ingredients are prepared and chopped before you start to cook this dish. You'll need a wok to cook the stir fry and it must be watched the whole time you are cooking. If you have to answer the phone or are interrupted, take the wok off the heat.

Serve your stir fry with rice or noodles and steamed spinach.

Serves 2–3

250g pork tenderloin, cut into 5mm slices

1 teaspoon soy sauce

½ teaspoon sugar

½ tablespoon vegetable oil

3cm piece fresh root ginger, finely chopped

4 spring onions, roughly sliced

1 garlic clove, finely chopped

1½ tablespoons oyster sauce

1½ tablespoons Hellmann's mayonnaise

Mix the pork with the soy sauce and the sugar. Pour the oil into the wok and heat up until it starts to smoke.

Add the pork pieces and brown for a couple of minutes on each side.

Add the ginger, spring onion and garlic. Fry on a moderate heat for another few minutes, stirring frequently.

Add 2 tablespoons water and the oyster sauce. Simmer for a couple of minutes, stirring frequently.

Finally, take the wok off the heat and stir in the Hellmann's until the sauce is smooth and creamy. The dish is ready.

GRILLED CORN SALSA WITH HELLMANN'S MAYONNAISE

You'll need to cook the corn on a barbecue to get an authentic flavour and attractive char-grilled look. This salsa is to be eaten immediately with freshly grilled burgers.

Serves 2

> 3 corn on the cob
>
> ½ red onion, finely chopped
>
> ⅓ cucumber, diced
>
> Handful of coriander, roughly chopped
>
> ½ teaspoon of Maldon sea salt
>
> Squirt of Tabasco pepper sauce
>
> Juice of ½ lime
>
> 2 heaped tablespoons Hellmann's mayonnaise

Cook the corn on a barbecue. Keep turning it until it is evenly charred but not overcooked. On an average barbecue this will take 10–15 minutes.

Let the corn cool enough so that you can handle it, then shave the kernels of corn off the cobs with a sharp knife. Place the cob upright on the chopping board and then cut downwards. Be carful when you do this.

Transfer the kernels of corn into a medium-size bowl. Add the onion, cucumber and coriander. Toss it around.

Sprinkle in the salt, Tabasco, lime juice and mayonnaise. Mix thoroughly.

This salsa should be made and eaten on the same day.

HEINZ BAKED BEANS

'Beanz Meanz Heinz', as the famous advertising jingle has it.

The slogan, which was dreamed up over a couple of pints in a pub in Mornington Crescent, was unleashed on the British public in 1967. Not that the people needed much convincing. They had been in love with Heinz baked beans ever since they were first sold at London's poshest shop in 1901. Fortnum & Mason still makes a point of carrying them, even if they can scarcely now be described as luxury items. But they are certainly valuable. The beans are so important to the HJ Heinz Company that only four employees are allowed to know the exact recipe at any one time.

It would be fair to say that the British are obsessed with baked haricot or navy beans, for those are the names of the bean in question. Some of the more eccentric manifestations of this obsession include fiercely contested world records for eating them individually with cocktail sticks (in 1981 Karen Stevenson of Merseyside managed 2780 in half an hour), and the habit of sitting in bath tubs full of cold beans to raise money for charity. But the biggest tribute to Heinz baked beans is probably the fact that they have become an essential component of the Great British Fry Up. There is something about their texture – firm yet yielding with a delectably mushy interior

– and the gently spicy tomato sauce in which they swim that makes them perfect companions to bacon, sausages and so on.

We could go on. A survey carried out by the University of Bath in 2005 revealed that Heinz baked beans was Britain's most popular branded food item bar none. In 1998, the beans and their famous turquoise-labelled cans were chosen as suitable items to go into a time capsule at the Business Design Centre in London. One and a half million tins are eaten in the UK every day. By now you've got the picture. Heinz baked beans may have been invented on the other side of the Atlantic but here they are regarded as a national food.

Interestingly, Heinz baked beans as the British know them are not generally available in the US. (The nearest equivalents are Heinz Premium Vegetarian Beans, which are darker, mushier, sweeter and nowhere near as popular.) A possible explanation for their absence is the American tradition of baking beans at home. New Englanders traditionally add maple syrup, while in the South they throw in some mustard plus bacon or ground beef. In either case, the beans are a great deal tangier and

more interesting than anything sold in a tin on that side of the Pond.

When it comes to recipes involving 'classic' Heinz baked beans, the possibilities are endless. We've even come across accounts of people eating them with ginger biscuits. That may be taking things a little too far, but they do go well with practically anything savoury. Their versatility and affordability makes them particularly popular with students. Few people can have attended college and missed out on the delights of baked bean chilli con carne or lasagne. The beans make a winning combo with cheese, and a spoonful or two will lift the most uncharismatic stew. But they are arguably at their best in the way they are most commonly eaten, namely with the sauce soaking into a slice of toasted bread. Among the following recipes you will therefore find one for the ultimate beans on toast.

BAKED BEAN CRUMBLE ON TOAST

This is an easy dish for one that elevates the humble beans and toast into another dimension. It shouldn't take more than 10 minutes to make.

Serves 1

3 slices fresh bread

1 heaped tablespoon grated mature Cheddar cheese

150g tin Heinz baked beans

Butter, for spreading

Maldon sea salt and freshly ground black pepper

Preheat the grill to medium.

Blend 1 of the slices of bread in the food processor by pulsing a couple of times. Combine the breadcrumbs with Cheddar, a couple of pinches of sea salt and a generous grind of pepper.

Toast the remaining bread under the grill. Heat up the beans in a small pan until piping hot. Place the toast on a grill tray and spread with butter.

Pour the beans onto the toast and top with the crumble mixture.

Grill for 5 minutes or so until the cheese is melted and the breadcrumbs are golden brown.

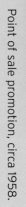

Point of sale promotion, circa 1958.

BAKED BEANS WITH HOMEMADE ITALIAN-STYLE MEATBALLS

We love meatballs, homemade ones with nice coarse mince and lots of herbs and garlic, served with chips or mashed potatoes. Nick considers this a man's dish which only hirsute individuals should be allowed to make, which is ironic as he's as bald as a billiard ball.

Serves 4

> 500g minced beef
>
> 1 small onion, finely chopped
>
> 3 garlic cloves, finely chopped
>
> Squirt of Tabasco pepper sauce
>
> A few drops of Lea & Perrins Worcestershire sauce
>
> 2 teaspoons dried mixed herbs (we use *herbes de Provence*)
>
> 2 teaspoons paprika
>
> Dribble of vegetable oil
>
> 2 x 415g tins Heinz baked beans
>
> 4 tablespoons water
>
> 2 tablespoons tomato purée
>
> Sprig or two of flat-leaf parsley, roughly chopped
>
> Salt and freshly ground black pepper

In a large bowl, place the beef, onion, garlic, Tabasco, Lea & Perrins, mixed herbs, paprika and seasoning. Mix them all together, squeezing and manipulating with your hands until it is a sticky mess. Form into meatballs with your fingers, any size you like.

Heat a little oil in a large frying pan on a moderate heat and fry the meatballs for about 8–10 minutes, turning so they are nicely browned all over.

Pour the beans, tomato purée and 4 tablespoons water into a saucepan. Stir until well combined, then add the browned meatballs. Simmer for about 5 minutes and then stir in the parsley. Serve immediately.

MASHED POTATOES WITH CHEESE, BEANS AND FRANKFURTERS

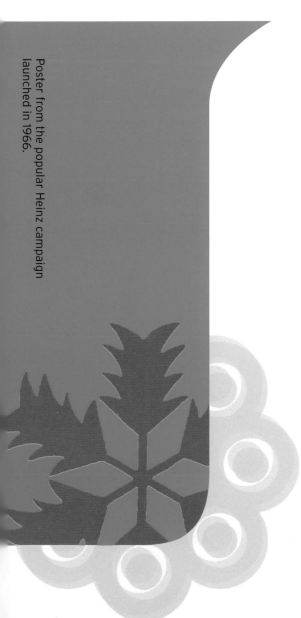

Nick spent several years in the doldrums, watching TV and preparing comfort food. This is one of the best recipes he devised during his wilderness period. You will need a small ovenproof dish. If you're feeling really lazy, you won't even need a plate.

Serves 1

- 2 medium-size potatoes, roughly sliced
- 1 tablespoon butter
- 1 teaspoon Colman's mustard
- 50g mature Cheddar cheese, grated
- 150g tin Heinz baked beans
- 2 frankfurters
- Salt and freshly ground black pepper

Preheat the oven to 220°C/425°F/gas mark 7.

Bring a medium-size pan of water to the boil and cook the diced potatoes for 15–20 minutes or until soft. Drain.

Add the butter, mustard and seasoning to the potatoes in the pan. Mash together with a fork.

Slice the frankfurters and mix with the beans. Transfer the beans and frankfurters into a small ovenproof dish. Spread the potato on top and sprinkle the cheese over. Bake for 20 minutes until golden brown.

To serve, eat in front of the TV. Do not answer the phone.

BAKED BEAN CASSOULET WITH CORNFLAKE CRUMBLE

✳✳✳✳✳✳✳✳✳✳✳✳✳✳✳✳✳✳✳✳✳✳✳✳✳✳✳✳✳✳✳✳✳✳

A cassoulet is a traditional sausage stew from southwest France. A Frenchman from Toulouse tasted our version of the delicacy. 'This is a wonderful modern interpretation of our cassoulet,' he crooned. Then Nick told him what was in it and watched him turn a lovely shade of crimson. For this recipe you will need a smallish dish that goes under the grill. We recommend you serve it with loads of crusty bread and a green salad.

Serves 2

6 Toulouse sausages

415g tin Heinz baked beans

½ teaspoon fennel seeds

Couple of sprigs of thyme, finely chopped

1 tablespoon tomato purée

1 chicken stock cube

3 tablespoons Kellogg's cornflakes

15g unsalted butter

4 sage leaves, finely chopped

Maldon sea salt and freshly ground black pepper

Fry the sausages in a pan until nicely browned.

Slice the browned sausages and tip them into a medium saucepan, followed by the baked beans, fennel seeds, thyme, tomato purée, crumbled stock cube and 4 tablespoons water. Simmer for 5 minutes, stirring occasionally.

Preheat the grill to medium.

Using the tips of your fingers, mix the cornflakes with the butter, sage and seasoning to form a crumbly paste.

Transfer the sausage and bean mixture to the serving dish and sprinkle over an even layer of crumb. Grill for 5–8 minutes until the crumb topping is nice and crispy. Serve immediately.

COTTAGE PIE
WITH HEINZ BAKED BEANS

This is comfort food at its best. With the addition of baked beans, a cottage pie makes a fabulous all-in-one supper or family lunch on a cold day.

Serves 4–6

1kg large potatoes, roughly diced

600g minced beef

1 tablespoon olive oil

3–4 garlic cloves, chopped

2 medium-size onions, chopped

3 medium-size carrots, chopped

250g mushrooms, chopped

1 beef stock cube

415g tin Heinz baked beans

2 tablespoons Heinz tomato ketchup

1 tablespoon Lea & Perrins Worcestershire sauce

A few sprigs of thyme, chopped

2 bay leaves

2 teaspoons Tabasco pepper sauce

25g unsalted butter

4 tablespoons milk

½ teaspoon ground nutmeg

Salt and freshly ground black pepper

Handful of grated Cheddar cheese

A few pinches of paprika

Preheat the oven to 200°C/400°F/ gas mark 6.

Bring a large pan of water to the boil and add the potatoes. Boil for 15–20 minutes, or until soft.

In a large frying pan or wok, fry the beef over a moderate to high heat, stirring constantly for around 5 minutes, until it has changed colour. Make sure the mince doesn't clump together.

Add the olive oil, garlic, onion, carrots and mushrooms to the pan. Continue to fry over a moderate heat, stirring frequently, for another 8–10 minutes until the vegetables are soft.

Add the crumbled stock cube, baked beans, tomato ketchup, Lea & Perrins, thyme, bay leaves and Tabasco, along with 250ml water. Simmer for a few minutes then taste and season if necessary.

Drain the potatoes. Mash with the butter, milk and nutmeg. Season with a little salt and pepper.

Spoon the mince into a large ovenproof dish. Carefully spread the mashed potato on top using a spatula or large spoon. Sprinkle the grated Cheddar on the potato plus a few pinches of paprika.

Bake for 35–40 minutes if you want to eat the pie straight away. You don't have to bake this dish immediately. You could keep it, covered, in the fridge for up to 24 hours but allow 45–50 minutes when you come to heat it up.

LEA & PERRINS WORCESTERSHIRE SAUCE

Many of the brands in this book are thoroughly palatable on their own. Lea & Perrins is different.

Unless you had a seriously jaded palate or a bizarre pregnancy craving, you wouldn't want to eat the stuff neat. But if you splash (or 'splish', as the manufacturers would have it) a little Lea & Perrins into a stew or a glass of tomato juice judiciously diluted with vodka, you will discover exactly what Worcestershire sauce is for. It imparts a glorious but non-specific savouriness that makes dishes that would otherwise be 'flat' burst into three dimensions. You don't want to overdo it though. If you're adding the correct amount to a recipe, you probably won't be able to taste it, at least directly. But your food will benefit enormously from it being there.

The origins of Worcestershire/Worcester sauce (the terms are interchangable) are shrouded in mythology which, it must be said, may include an element of marketing baloney. The one thing we can be sure of is that it was created during the mid-1830s by a pair of Worcester chemists called John Lea (1791–1874) and William Perrins (1793–1867). According to one version of events, a homesick Maharajah popped into their pharmacy in the English Midlands and asked them to knock up a sauce that would remind him of India. The Lea & Perrins website goes with the theory that the story began when a Lord Sandys returned home from a tour of Bengal and asked the creators to duplicate a recipe he had picked up on his travels. Lea & Perrins are said to have obliged but found the resulting sauce so disgusting that they put the sample jars in the cellar and forgot all about them. Only when they found them some years later did they discover that the contents had matured into something delectable.

Initially, via word of mouth alone, the Lea & Perrins habit spread rapidly through Europe and thence to the rest of the world. The founders shrewdly adopted a tactic of 'placing' the sauce on ocean liners departing from Britain. They even paid the stewards to serve it. By 1839, Worcester sauce had arrived in America, where it proved so popular that the importer, John Duncan, built a factory to manufacture it locally. Before long, Lea & Perrins was cropping up in the most far-flung places. In 1904, Lieutenant-Colonel Sir Francis Edward Young arrived in the forbidden city of Llahsa after an arduous journey. Some Tibetan monks took pity on him and served him a meal. There on the table was a bottle of Lea & Perrins.

Worcester sauce is now truly global. *Salsa inglesa,* as it is known in Spanish speaking nations, is a crucial ingredient in Peruvian *ceviche* and the Mexican beer cocktail Michelada. If you order dim sum in Hong Kong, your steamed meatballs will invariably arrive with a dish of Lea & Perrins. The Japanese, meanwhile, have created an anchovy-free Worcester sauce of their own. Called *shosu* (sauce) or *ustah* (Worcester), it is the standard accompaniment for *tonkatsu* (breaded pork loin).

When we consider the indirect ancestry of this potent concoction of anchovies, onions, shallots, garlic, malt vinegar, tamarind, cloves, chillies and molasses, its universal appeal starts to make sense. Fermented fish sauces have been popular since time immemorial. Lea & Perrins is not only a direct cousin of the likes of Thai *nam prik pla;* it is the modern equivalent of garum, the definitive flavouring of the Roman Empire.

LOBSTER WITH LEA & PERRINS

Lobsters have got so many bits and pieces that they can be scary to cook. Our advice is to buy one that is already boiled, leaving you with one less thing to do at home.

Serves 2

1 small to medium-size cooked lobster

1 tablespoon unsalted butter

1 large shallot, finely chopped

1 glass white wine

1 tablespoon Lea & Perrins Worcestershire sauce

1 tablespoon tomato purée

3 tablespoons double cream

Juice of ½ lemon

Small handful flat-leaf parsley, roughly chopped

2 tablespoons grated Parmesan cheese

Preheat the oven to 200°C/400°F/ gas mark 6.

Look the lobster up and down. You will see that it is composed of a tail and head with lots of large and small appendages in-between. Turn the lobster onto its back. You can leave all the sticky-out bits attached, but rip off the claws. Try to extract as much meat as possible from them; pliers will help.

As you will have noticed, the lobster will still be lying on its back in exactly the same position, but looking slightly less scary as it will be missing its claws. Using a sharp knife (and be VERY careful), cut into its soft (er) belly and cut from head to tail lengthways, then splay open.

Take out all the meat, including the gooey sloppy bits. Chop up all the lobster meat and replace into the shell.

To make the sauce, heat the butter in a small pan and gently fry the shallot for a few minutes until soft, then add the wine, Lea & Perrins and tomato purée. Simmer until the sauce has become quite thick.

Add the double cream, lemon juice and parsley to the sauce. Boil for another couple of minutes. Set aside to cool for 10 minutes.

Pour the sauce onto the lobster and top with the grated Parmesan. Bake in the oven for 15 minutes until golden brown on top.

SAUSAGE HOTPOT WITH LEA & PERRINS

This is a chuck-it-in-the-pot hotpot but certainly not a hope-for-the-best one. You can keep it in the fridge for a few days and if anything its flavour will improve. Serve with plenty of crusty bread and butter.

Serves 4

- 400g pork sausages
- 1 tablespoon butter
- 1 medium-size onion, roughly diced
- 1 leek, roughly chopped
- 2 garlic cloves, chopped
- 2 teaspoons paprika
- 1 medium-size red pepper, roughly diced
- 2 tablespoons tomato purée
- 1 large glass red wine
- 1–2 sprigs thyme, chopped
- 2 fresh bay leaves
- 3 medium-size potatoes, roughly diced
- 400g tin chopped tomatoes
- 1 tablespoon Lea & Perrins Worcestershire sauce
- 2 beef stock cubes

Fry or grill the sausages until nice and browned. Leave on the side to cool. Slice into discs.

Melt the butter in a large saucepan. Gently fry the onion, leek, garlic, paprika and red pepper for 10 minutes or so.

Add the tomato purée, wine, thyme, bay leaves, potatoes, tomatoes, Lea & Perrins and crumbled stock cubes, along with 600ml water. Finally, throw in the sliced sausages.

Simmer for 30 minutes or until the potatoes are cooked.

BEEF RAGU WITH HEINZ KETCHUP AND LEA & PERRINS

If you ask for 'bolognese' in Bologna, the locals tend to look a bit nonplussed. This is because the Italians know the sauce as *ragu*. This is a simple but luxurious tasting version that goes down well with children and adults alike. It is best cooked in a wok or large frying pan. Just for a change we recommend serving it with mashed potato.

Serves 2

Splash of olive oil

300g beef fillet, cut into strips

1 tablespoon butter

2 medium-size shallots, peeled and sliced

150g mushrooms, sliced

2 teaspoons Lea & Perrins Worcestershire sauce

2 tablespoons Heinz tomato ketchup

150ml crème fraîche

Sprig or two of flat-leaf parsley, roughly chopped

Heat the olive oil in a wok or large frying pan and fry the beef over a high heat for about 3 minutes. Using a slotted spoon, remove the beef from the pan and set aside.

Add the butter to the pan. When melted, add the shallots and fry over a gentle heat for 5 minutes, stirring frequently.

Add the mushrooms to the pan. Continue to cook for another 5 minutes or so until the mushrooms are cooked through.

Return the beef to the pan and add the Lea & Perrins, ketchup and crème fraîche. Simmer for a few minutes.

Garnish with the parsley and serve.

TABASCO PEPPER SAUCE

You could be forgiven for thinking that Tabasco pepper sauce was made in the Mexican state of that name.

In fact, it comes from Avery Island in Louisiana, where the family-run McIlhenny Company has been making it for seven generations. The variety of pepper used in the original pepper sauce formula is also called 'tabasco'. Tabasco works well as a brand name as it conjures up images of extreme heat.

Avery Island is an interesting place. Lying in the middle of a grassy marshland, it is essentially a huge dome of salt. The local Native Americans were exploiting this resource and trading it throughout the South long before the arrival of European settlers. The presence of salt is also a major boon from the Tabasco perspective as it is one of only three ingredients used in the production of the sauce. The other two are hot peppers (as you might expect) and grain vinegar.

According to one McIlhenny family legend, the Tabasco story began when a soldier returning from the US-Mexican War of 1846–1848 gave a New Orleans banker named Edmund McIlhenny a handful of dried red chillies. McIlhenny enjoyed eating them so much that he kept the seeds and planted them in the garden of his home on Avery Island. His agricultural activities, however,

were interrupted by the Civil War. In 1863, Union forces invaded the island to get their hands on its salt mines, forcing McIlhenny and his family to flee to Texas. When McIlhenny returned to the island, he found growing on it a single pepper plant.

McIlhenny was understandably desperate to make a profit from his one surviving crop. Accordingly, he developed the sauce that would bring him fame and fortune. Then he poured it into empty cologne bottles and dispatched them to prospective customers. Soon, a major New York grocery firm, EC Hazard and Company, began to distribute McIlhenny's sauce, helping the fiery condiment to become famous throughout the US.

Tabasco has enjoyed various PR coups during its lifetime. A reporter spotted it for sale on the upper Nile when travelling with Lord Kitchener on his campaign to retake Khartoum in 1897. Then there was the 'Tabasco Tempest' of 1932, in which Members of Parliament argued about the presence of the sauce in the House of Commons dining rooms during a 'Buy British' campaign. Another defining moment in Tabasco's entry into global consciousness occurred at the King Cole Bar at the St Regis Hotel

in New York around 1935. A bartender called Fernand 'Pete' Petiot decided to add a few drops to a glass of vodka and tomato juice, and the Bloody Mary as we know it today was born.

The way in which Avery Island's most famous product is made has scarcely changed since its invention. The only difference is that the maturation period has been substantially extended. As soon as the ripe peppers are picked, they are mashed up with a little salt and placed in white oak barrels. There they remain for up to three years. Then, when a member of the McIlhenny family deems the time is right, they are mixed with vinegar. After four weeks of regular stirring the mixture is strained to remove the seeds and skins and then bottled. Voila!

HOT AND SOUR SOUP WITH TABASCO

This is a quick and easy recipe for a refreshing, slightly spicy starter. It's only marginally more demanding than making a cup-a-soup. If you want to give it slightly more body, try adding some prawns or vegetables.

Serves 4

- **2 chicken stock cubes**
- **2 tablespoons cider vinegar**
- **2 teaspoons Tabasco pepper sauce**
- **Juice of ½ lime**
- **2cm piece fresh root ginger, finely chopped**
- **2 spring onions, sliced**
- **1 chicken breast, thinly sliced**

Heat up 750ml water in a saucepan. Add the rest of the ingredients.

Simmer for 5 minutes and the soup is ready to serve.

THE LITTLE PEPPER UPPER.

1990s magazine advert.

This soup should be prepared in advance as it is served chilled. With its deep ruby body and creamy swirl it's a feast for both your eyes and stomach. It makes a great starter on a hot day.

Serves 4

BORSCHT WITH TABASCO-SPICED SWIRL

For the soup

2 medium-size beetroot (350–400g), roughly chopped

2 medium-size potatoes (300g), chopped

2 beef or vegetable stock cubes

2 tablespoons balsamic vinegar

4 tablespoons vodka

1 tablespoon tomato purée

For the swirl

2 tablespoons double cream

2 teaspoons Tabasco pepper sauce

For the croûtons

2 slices of bread, cut into small squares

1 teaspoon mixed herbs

Freshly ground black pepper

Pinch of Maldon sea salt

Splash of olive oil

To make the soup, combine all the soup ingredients, along with 750ml water, in a pan. Bring to the boil, then simmer for 30 minutes until all the vegetables are soft. If the soup looks a little sludgy during the latter stages of cooking, top it up with water. Finely blend the soup with a hand blender. Allow to cool, then refrigerate until it is needed.

Mix together the swirl ingredients.

For the croûtons, place the bread squares in a bowl, then add the mixed herbs, some black pepper and sea salt. Toss around until the croûtons are coated. Just prior to serving, heat the olive oil in a frying pan and gently fry the croûtons until golden brown (approximately 10 minutes).

****

To serve the soup, divide it among 4 soup bowls and give each portion a swirl of Tabasco-spiced cream. To do this, take a blob on a tablespoon, tilt the spoon slightly over the centre of the soup bowl and pour it in gently as you move the spoon around in ever increasing circles.

Garnish with the warm, toasted croûtons. Serve immediately; don't wait until the soup has warmed up!

SPICY TABBOULEH WITH HERBS

****

A few simple ingredients can transform plain bulgur wheat into a really special side dish. This tabbouleh is fantastic with grilled or barbecued lamb.

Serves 4

125g bulgur wheat

1 tablespoon olive oil

25g flat-leaf parsley, roughly chopped

25g mint, roughly chopped

Juice of 1 lemon

2 teaspoons Tabasco pepper sauce

½ teaspoon Maldon sea salt

4 tomatoes, chopped

Cook the bulgur wheat according to the pack instructions and rinse under cold running water to cool. Drain thoroughly.

Dress the bulgur wheat with the olive oil. Mix thoroughly. Stir in the remaining ingredients and chill until ready to serve.

TABASCO-SEASONED PRAWNS WITH TOMATO SAUCE

This dish has a spicy Latin feel and takes only a few minutes to make. Rice makes a good accompaniment.

Serves 2

1 tablespoon olive oil

1 red pepper, sliced

2 garlic cloves, chopped

1 medium-size onion, sliced

200g raw peeled prawns

2 teaspoons ground *pimentón* (Spanish ground red chilli) or paprika

Half a 295g tin Campbell's condensed cream of tomato soup

2 teaspoons Tabasco pepper sauce

1 teaspoon dried mixed herbs

Heat the olive oil in a large frying pan. Fry the red pepper, garlic, onion and prawns over a high heat, stirring constantly for a few minutes.

Add the *pimentón* or paprika and carry on cooking for a further minute. Add the Campbell's soup, Tabasco, 4 tablespoons water and the mixed herbs and simmer for a few minutes.

GRILLED MONKFISH WITH TABASCO AND LIME

This is an exceptionally light dish, with sour flavours that are very Thai. You wouldn't want to meet a whole monkfish on a dark night but its flesh is delicious, low in fat and surprisingly meat-like. Serve with rice or noodles.

Serves 2

300g monkfish, cut into chunks

1 red pepper, cut into chunks

1 medium-size red onion, cut into chunks

Large sprig of coriander, roughly chopped

Juice of 1 lime

2 teaspoons Tabasco pepper sauce

1 tablespoon sesame oil

1 tablespoon fish sauce

Preheat the grill to high.

Combine all the ingredients in a shallow grill tray. Toss them around so that they are all coated with the lovely flavours.

Grill on full heat for 10–12 minutes, turning the fish chunks after 5 minutes, until the red peppers are charred at the edges and a lovely sour sauce appears at the bottom of the dish.

A series of of old Tabasco advertisements dating back to 1900.

Nick was in the South of France when he created this dish. The surroundings inspired him to throw in some *herbes de Provence,* a mixture of aromatic herbs from the region that is widely available in supermarkets. His French neighbours were delighted with the result, something that is far from guaranteed when people of that nationality eat food prepared by English cooks. Serve with Tabasco spicy potatoes (see right).

SPICED BBQ GLAZED CHICKEN

Serves 4

- 2 garlic cloves, finely chopped
- 1 tablespoon dried *herbes de Provence*
- 1 teaspoon Maldon sea salt
- Juice of 1 lime
- 2 teaspoons clear honey
- 3 teaspoons Tabasco pepper sauce
- 2 teaspoons paprika
- 2 teaspoons Lea & Perrins Worcestershire sauce
- 1 tablespoon balsamic vinegar
- Splash of olive oil
- Little squirt of Heinz tomato ketchup
- 8–10 chicken pieces (such as drumsticks and thighs)

Mix all the ingredients, except the chicken, in a jug and stir well. Arrange the chicken in a single layer in a large ovenproof dish and pour the marinade over. Leave the chicken to marinate for an hour or so.

Preheat the oven to 160°C/325°F/ gas mark 3. Roast the chicken for 45–50 minutes, then serve.

TABASCO SPICY POTATOES

This dish is essentially a spicier version of Spanish *patatas bravas*. It works equally well as a starter, snack or accompaniment to a main course. Since you will already have got the Tabasco pepper sauce out, there's a strong case for the latter to be spiced BBQ glazed chicken (see left). You will need a large frying pan.

Serves 4

For the dip

    4 tablespoons Hellmann's
    mayonnaise

    4 teaspoons Tabasco pepper sauce

    Juice of 1 lime

For the potatoes

    8 medium-size potatoes, scrubbed,
    unpeeled and roughly diced

    Handful of thyme leaves, stripped
    off stalk

    3 teaspoons Tabasco pepper sauce

    1 teaspoon Maldon sea salt

    2 teaspoons paprika

    2 garlic cloves, finely chopped

    Juice of ½ lime

    2 tablespoons vegetable oil

Make the dip by combining the ingredients in a small bowl using a fork or a little whisk.

Parboil the potatoes, in a pan of boiling water, for a maximum of 10 minutes. They need to be slightly hard so that they don't fall apart when you sauté them. While they are boiling, mix the thyme, Tabasco, sea salt, paprika, garlic and lime together in a small bowl.

Drain the potatoes, place them in a large bowl and gently coat them with the seasoning mixture.

Heat up the oil in the pan and fry the potatoes, turning frequently, until nicely browned. Serve the potatoes with the spicy dip.

KIKKOMAN SOY SAUCE

Scientists once believed that humans could distinguish four fundamental flavours, but in recent years, evidence has mounted for the existence of a fifth.

In addition to receptors for sweet, sour, salt and bitter, the tongue is now thought to contain one responsible for the lip-smacking tang associated with savoury foods. Perhaps revealingly, English lacks a term for the sensation in question, but the Japanese have long had a word for it. They call it *umami* and *umami* is what Kikkoman soy sauce is all about.

The literal translation of Kikkoman is 'turtle shell ten thousand'. In line with this, the company logo consists of *man*, the character for 'ten thousand', sitting inside a hexagonal shape designed to represent a turtle shell. This emphasis on an aquatic reptile may seem a trifle curious for a brand of soy sauce, but with a little background knowledge it starts to make sense. The Japanese believe the turtle (*ki*) to be extremely long-lived (legend has it that its lifespan is 10,000 years) and therefore regard it as a lucky symbol. *Ko,* meanwhile, the second part of the name for its shell, means 'top quality'. The cumulative message of Kikkoman is therefore 'propitious and top quality substance that will be around for an awfully long time'. When you taste the sauce and consider its history, this seems an entirely fair description.

Kikkoman is one of the oldest food brands in the world. The name has been in use since 1782, but the origins of the company stretch back at least another 120 years. In the 1600s, an ancestor of the current CEO started to brew *shoyu* (soy sauce) in the town of Noda, about 30 miles upriver from modern Tokyo. Then, as now, it was made with just four ingredients – soya beans, wheat, salt and water – plus an all-important starter culture to produce the enzymes responsible for transforming them. Wheat starch is converted into sugar, some of which then turns to the alcohol and related substances that give the sauce its characteristic aroma. Meanwhile, some of the soya bean protein is broken down to its constituent amino acids. The result is, well, *umami.*

The *shoyu* that emerges after six months of fermentation is complex (experts can distinguish almost 300 separate aromas in Kikkoman soy sauce) yet thoroughly harmonious. Above all, it is extremely yummy. To convince yourself of the superiority of Kikkoman, we suggest you perform a simple experiment. Pour a little into a dish and do the same with a competing brand that lists caramel as one of its ingredients. Chances are that the latter will be 'non-brewed', i.e.

chemically produced with hydrochloric acid taking the role of the enzymes. Then have a slurp from each dish and compare the two experiences. You will almost certainly find that the Kikkoman is smoother, purer, initially sweeter and totally without the rival's harshness or bitter aftertaste.

Fortunately, identifying Kikkoman on the shop shelf is child's play. Like many of the world's great food brands, its packaging is unmistakable. Since 1961, the sauce has been sold in a sexily bulging bottle with a natty red top. It was created by Kenji Ekuan, a man responsible for several other Japanese design icons including the Bullet Train.

So how should you use Kikkoman soy sauce? In Asia, it is employed as an all-purpose seasoning and flavour enhancer, rather like salt and pepper in the West. It also makes a great marinade and a superlative dipping sauce. And Kikkoman is ideal for basting purposes. If you paint some onto roasting meat or fish, it will produce an attractive and very tasty glaze. Just make sure you seal the bottle properly when you're finished. As with all fermented products, too much exposure to air will cause Kikkoman soy sauce to deteriorate.

DUCK BREAST WITH CASHEWS AND KIKKOMAN SOY SAUCE

* *

This is tasty, spicy and eye-catching, and takes very little preparation. Serve with noodles and your favourite steamed green veg for a speedy supper.

Serves 2

2 duck breasts, skin on

2 tablespoons Kikkoman soy sauce

Couple of splashes of Tabasco pepper sauce

2 handfuls cashew nuts

Juice of ½ lime

4 spring onions, chopped

Handful of coriander, roughly chopped

Preheat the oven to 160°C/325°F/ gas mark 3.

Lightly score the skin of the duck breasts with a knife. Season the breasts with 1 tablespoon soy sauce and a splash of Tabasco.

Place the cashews on a baking tray and roast for 10 minutes.

Gently fry the duck breasts in a non-stick pan, skin side down, for 10 minutes. Pour off the excess fat and continue to fry on the other side for a further 10 minutes.

Remove the breasts from the pan and set aside in a warm place to rest for a few minutes, then slice and place in a bowl.

Add the remaining tablespoon of soy sauce to the bowl with a splash of Tabasco, the lime juice, spring onions, cashews and coriander. Toss around to combine all the ingredients and serve.

FENNEL AND ORANGE SPICED CHICKEN WITH KIKKOMAN SOY SAUCE

We've used chicken thighs and drumsticks in this flavour-packed dish as they tend to stay moist and succulent. Serve with rice or noodles.

Serves 4

1 fennel bulb, thinly sliced

8 chicken thighs and drumsticks

2 tablespoons Kikkoman soy sauce

2 teaspoons clear honey

2.5cm piece fresh root ginger, thinly sliced

Juice and zest of 1 orange

1 teaspoon five-spice powder

1 tablespoon sesame oil

Preheat the oven to 200°C/400°F/ gas mark 6.

Choose a casserole dish large enough to take all the chicken pieces. Throw in all the ingredients and mix thoroughly.

By the time you have finished mixing, make sure that the fennel is nestling at the bottom of the dish.

Bake for 40 minutes, then serve.

Japanese engraving dating back to around 1600, showing the process of making soy sauce.

GUINNESS

During the late 18th century, a new kind of beer became popular among the porters in and around London's Covent Garden.

It was made with roasted barley and was much darker than traditional ale. As a result of its core fan base, it became known as 'porter'. Arthur Guinness was quick to spot the new trend, and in 1799 made the momentous decision to make the new drink the focus of his brewing operation. It wasn't a bad choice. Today the firm sells more than two billion pints of porter/stout (the terms are virtually interchangeable) per year.

Interestingly, Guinness came within a whisker of never having existed. In 1775, following a dispute about a proposed water levy, the Dublin Corporation sent a gang of labourers to fill in the water course feeding Arthur Guinness's brewery at St James' Gate. Guinness, who 16 years earlier had purchased a lease on the site that appeared to guarantee him free water for 9,000 years, was having none of that. He grabbed a pick-axe, swore copiously at the men and chased them away. Eventually, he reached an agreement with the Corporation that secured the brewery access to 'liquor' (pure water) from the St James' Wells in the Wicklow Mountains until the year 10759. The way was now clear for the creation of Ireland's national drink.

So what is the secret of Guinness? Well, for one thing, it is highly appealing to the senses. Visually, a correctly poured pint is a treat. First there is the 'surge', when the unique mixture of nitrogen and carbon dioxide in the drink is released, causing it to swirl hypnotically. Then the contents separate into the luscious dark body and creamy head that have earned Guinness the nickname of 'the blonde in the black dress'. When you finally get to imbibe the drink, the first thing to strike you may be its smooth texture. Nitrogen produces much smaller bubbles than the carbon dioxide present in most fizzy drinks, hence the thick creamy head and full-bodied mouth feel. Some have likened the experience to drinking a steak. Finally, we come to the bottom line, the taste. Words begin to fail at this point, but let's just say Guinness is rich, strong and satisfying.

Aside from the company's long tradition of producing wonderful adverts, the final explanation for Guinness's popularity is its reputation for being healthy. 'Guinness is good for you', the ads used to proclaim during the 1920s. In today's climate, in which the official line is that nothing containing alcohol can possibly be good for you, it is no longer prudent or even possible for the manufacturers

to make this claim. But provided it is consumed in moderation, might there not be some truth in the old slogan? Recent research suggests that there might. Apparently, the drink hinders the formation of clots in the blood. It certainly contains antioxidants. Whatever the truth of the matter, the notion that Guinness is good for you persists. It is still prescribed for post-operative patients, nursing mothers and blood donors in Ireland. Some landlords in the Emerald Isle go as far as calling it 'Vitamin G'.

Fortunately, we can stay out of the debate because most, if not all, the alcohol in Guinness evaporates when it is used as a cooking ingredient. All you need to know when cooking with Guinness is that it is rich, nutritious and very tasty. It's robust so it stands up well to stewing and will give body and depth to many a recipe. Guinness can be a little bitter for some palates though. If this applies to you, you can counteract the effect with a bit of brown sugar.

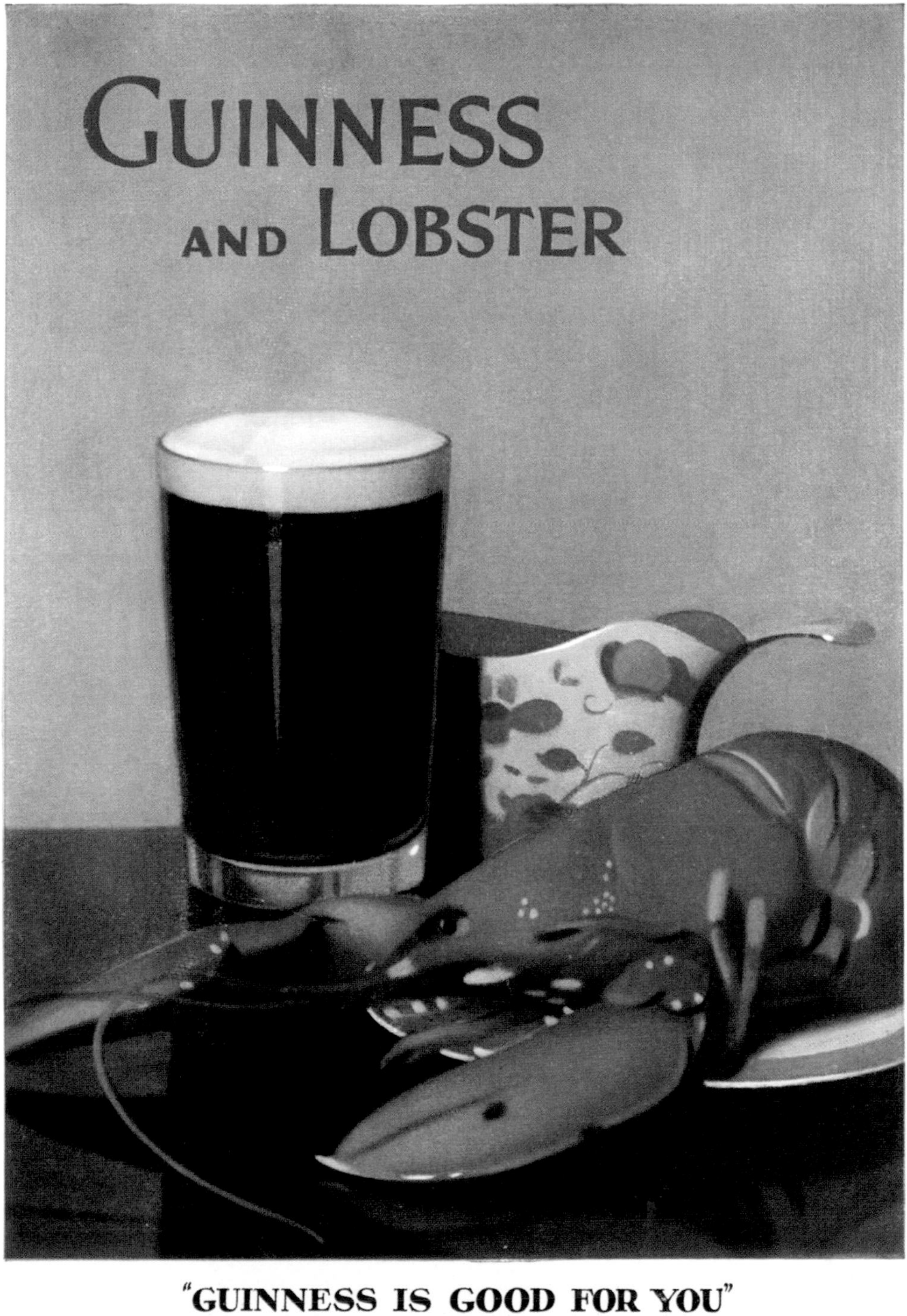
GUINNESS
AND LOBSTER
"GUINNESS IS GOOD FOR YOU"

CREAM OF GUINNESS AND ONION SOUP

With its black body and white top, this soup looks pleasingly like a pint of Guinness. To emphasise the point, serve it in small tankards or glass coffee cups. It makes an excellent dinner party starter.

Serves 4

50g butter

500g onions, sliced

1 tablespoon soft dark brown sugar

2 tablespoons Heinz tomato ketchup

Drop or two of Tabasco pepper sauce

Splash of Lea & Perrins Worcestershire sauce

400ml Guinness

2 beef stock cubes

100ml double cream

Melt the butter in a saucepan. Add the onions and sugar. Caramelise gently over a low heat for 20 minutes, until the onions are soft.

Add the ketchup, Tabasco, Lea & Perrins, Guinness and stock cubes.

Half fill the empty Guinness can with water and pour this into the soup as well. Simmer for 20 minutes.

Just before the soup is ready, whisk the cream until it is thickened but still runny. This is important as you are going to pour it on top of the soup to look like the froth on a pint of Guinness.

Carefully pour the soup into the glasses and top with the cream.

COCA-COLA

According to Interbrand, the research company best placed to know these things, Coca-Cola is the most valuable brand in the world.

If you leave out 'tangible assets' like real estate, the trademark is currently worth a shade over $65 billion. So what is it about this fizzy brown drink that has allowed it to achieve global domination?

Let's start by dispensing with a couple of urban myths. If Coke's success was down to the sugar and caffeine it contains, it would be hard to account for the permanent presence of the diet and caffeine-free varieties in the soft drinks Top 10. And the popularity of the drink certainly can't be explained by the fact that it has cocaine in it, because it doesn't.

Two factors explain why Coca-Cola is the world's most popular soft drink: inherent excellence and brilliant marketing. To convince yourself of the former, just watch someone drinking his or her first glass of Coke. It's sweet and bubbly, it tastes like nothing else in the world (apart from its usually pale imitators) and it's black! Meanwhile, to appreciate the contribution of ingenious promotion to Coca-Cola's success, a brief history lesson is in order.

Coca-Cola was invented in Atlanta, Georgia in May 1886 by a pharmacist named John Pemberton. He mixed up the ingredients in a three-legged brass kettle in his back yard. Then he nipped round the corner to the Jacob's Pharmacy and got the proprietor to add some carbonated water to his caramel-coloured syrup. Customers at the pharmacy's soda fountain found the result extremely palatable. Pemberton's bookkeeper Frank Robinson suggested the name 'Coca-Cola' for the new drink and wrote it out in the flowing script that still adorns the bottles and cans.

Sales in the first year of Coke's existence were sluggish to say the least – nine servings a day as opposed to a billion-odd today – but that changed dramatically when Pemberton sold out to another Atlanta-born pharmacist named Asa Candler. He relentlessly promoted Coca-Cola, dispensing coupons for free tastings and giving branded paraphernalia to cafés and soda fountains for free.

The success of Coca-Cola inevitably spawned a rash of copycat brands. Candler's response was to surround the formula for the syrup ('7X') with a secrecy that would put MI5 or the CIA to shame. To this day, no one employee is privy to the full list of ingredients, and the few who know part of the story are not allowed to travel on the same plane in case it crashes.

It was during the Second World War that Coca-Cola went truly global. When the US entered the war in 1941, the company's president Robert Woodruff announced that 'every man in uniform gets a bottle of Coca-Cola for 5 cents, wherever he is, and whatever it costs the Company'. The results of these efforts not only cheered up the GIs; it also gave millions of non-Americans their first taste of the 'black gold'.

The post-war marketing of Coca-Cola has been characterised by the introduction of Diet Coke and by memorable advertising slogans like 'The Real Thing'. In 1985, the company took the now insane-seeming decision to change the formula, but the introduction of New Coke just served to remind customers how much they loved the old stuff.

'Classic' Coke makes an excellent cooking ingredient. It may be tempting from a calorific perspective to use Diet Coke in some recipes but the results are likely to be disappointing. A nameless lady (clue: she's married to Johnny) once baked a ham in Diet Coca-Cola. Her intentions were worthy but it tasted pretty weird to the assembled diners. If she had used the regular variety the meat would have been deliciously caramelised.

BUBBLE TEA WITH COCA-COLA

Bubble tea is a South East Asian phenomenon that involves adding tapioca pearls to sweet drinks. It's a texture thing; the pearls don't have much flavour but they provide a lovely mouth sensation as you suck them up the straw.

Tapioca pearls come in all shapes, sizes and colours. Our favourite type for this drink is a small pearl flavoured with rosella (extracted from a type of hibiscus plant) to give it a light pink colour. We're also fond of the green ones that are flavoured with pandan leaf. Many kinds of tapioca pearls are available in Asian supermarkets so take your pick.

The one problem we've identified with bubble teas is that not many of them contain alcohol. This cocktail rectifies the situation. Obviously, you can leave the vodka out for an alcohol-free version of this drink.

For this cocktail you will need a tumbler and drinking straws.

Serves 1

2 teaspoons tapioca pearls

1 cup of black Earl Grey tea, cooled

4 ice cubes

1 generous shot of vodka

I can Coca-Cola

1 lemon, sliced

Follow the packet instructions to cook the tapioca pearls, then pop them in a bowl of cold water to stop them from sticking together.

Pour about 2–3cm Earl Grey into a tumbler, followed by the ice cubes. Add the vodka, followed by enough Coca-Cola to reach within 2.5cm of the top. Push in 4 slices of lemon, giving each one a little squeeze as it goes in.

Lastly, drain the tapioca pearls and carefully place them on top; they will gently float down like phosphorescence in the inky black. Add straws and the drink is ready.

Advertisement, 1954.

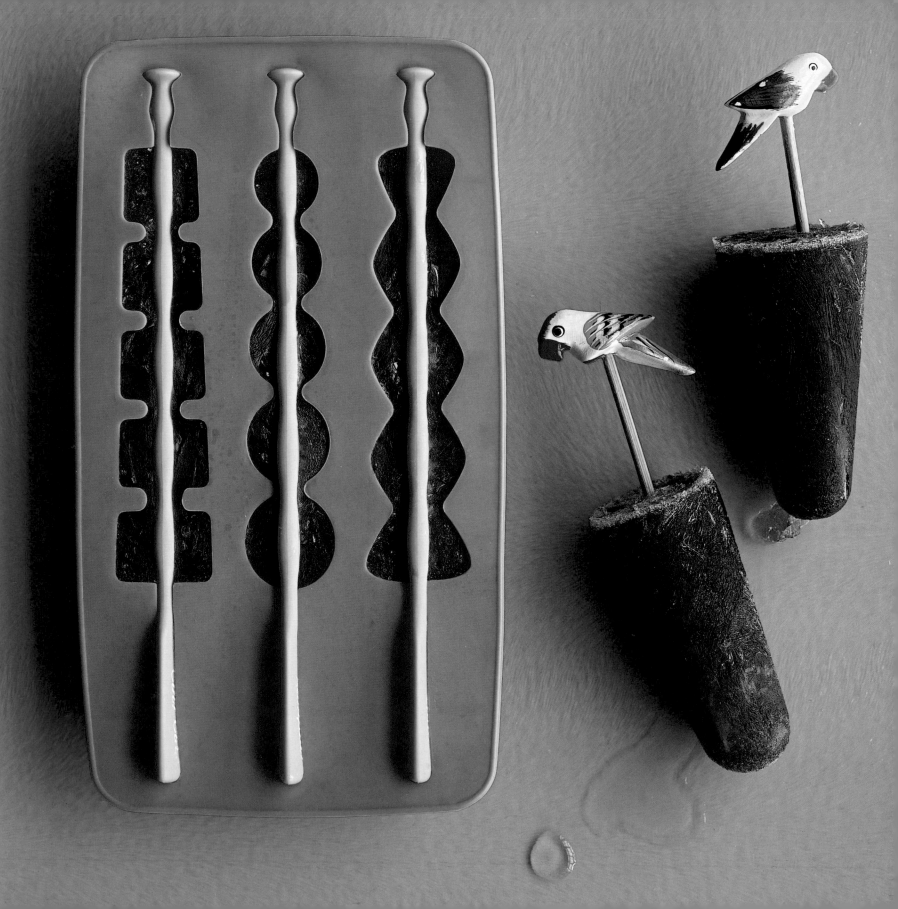

CUBA LIBRE ICE LOLLIES

The name Cuba Libre ('free Cuba') is politically contentious in its native land, but there is no doubt that rum, Coke and lime juice combine to make an excellent cocktail. It is particularly good when frozen, which is what inspired us to make it into ice lollies. They are tangy, remarkably refreshing and take but a few minutes to knock up. Try serving them in-between courses at a dinner party, possibly with some salsa music on in the background.

This recipe gives the proportions for small lollies that we would recommend for beginners. If you need more of the mixture, simply double or triple the quantities. You will need some ice lolly moulds.

Makes 3–4 lollies

100ml Coca-Cola
25ml dark rum
Juice of ½ lime

Gently mix the liquids together, not too much or you'll lose the fizz. Pour into the moulds and freeze until frozen.

FROTHY COCA-COLA AND BANANA CAKE

This cake, with its delightful frothy topping, is at least as good as it sounds. To make it, you will need an electric mixer, a sugar thermometer and a cake tin approximately 22–24cm in diameter. You will also need a small heavy-based saucepan because you are going to melt some sugar. Don't be scared by this – it's easy.

Serves 4

For the cake

> 3 medium eggs
>
> 100g soft light brown sugar
>
> 75ml Coca-Cola
>
> 150g self-raising flour
>
> 150g ground almonds
>
> A few drops of vanilla extract
>
> 3 large bananas, well mashed
>
> 75g butter, melted, plus extra for greasing

For the froth

> 4 medium egg whites
>
> Pinch of salt
>
> 1 teaspoon cream of tartar
>
> 100ml Coca-Cola
>
> 200g soft light brown sugar

Preheat the oven to 160°C/325°F/gas mark 3. Grease the cake tin or line it with greaseproof paper.

To make the cake, beat the eggs, sugar and Coca-Cola in a mixer set to high speed for 5 minutes. You want the mixture to be completely frothed up.

Gently fold in the flour, almonds and vanilla extract with a spatula. Then fold in the mashed banana, followed by the cooled melted butter. Transfer the mixture into the prepared cake tin.

Bake in the oven for 45 minutes. Remove from the tin and leave to cool on a wire rack.

To make the froth, beat the egg whites, salt and cream of tartar in the mixer, again at high speed, until whisked up into soft peaks. Leave the froth in the mixer while you melt the sugar. To do this, add the Coca-Cola to the sugar in a small saucepan, then heat gently until the liquid reaches 116°C/240°F (or what is known as 'soft ball stage'), stirring continuously. Do not perform any other kitchen activities while you are doing this – it needs your undivided attention.

Now turn the mixer back on, but this time on a slow setting. Slowly pour most of the melted sugar into the whisked egg whites.

Now put the lid on the mixture and turn it up to full speed. After you have whisked the froth for a minute or two, it should have the consistency of spreadable polystyrene (if such a thing existed!). Spread the froth evenly over the cooled cake, pulling it into artful peaks.

This cake is best eaten within a few hours of making it, but will keep for 24 hours in the fridge.

CAMP COFFEE

Mention Camp coffee to some people who were around during World War II and their eyes will mist over with tears of nostalgia.

Younger folk, on the other hand, may have no idea what you are talking about. ('They don't know what they're missing', as the farmer's wife who lived across the field from Johnny would say as she made him a glass when he was little). But the product in question, a unique bottled concoction of coffee, chicory and sugar in that order of concentration, is still alive and available. What's more, it has recently become a chic cooking ingredient employed by Michelin-starred chefs.

Camp coffee, now owned by McCormick (UK) Ltd, was invented in 1885 by a Glasgow food company called Robert Paterson & Sons. The spur to its creation was a demand among Scottish soldiers on campaign in India for a coffee-based drink that could be prepared easily and quickly in the field. As the Scots are, by their own admission, an economically minded race, it is no great surprise that Paterson & Sons came up with a clever way of eking out the then expensive commodity of coffee. They mixed it with essence of chicory, the bitter salad vegetable also known as endive. Then, to counteract the bitterness, they added a great deal of sugar. The result was a treacly brown syrup that could be mixed with either cold or hot milk to make a splendidly refreshing drink. Or at least

it was splendid once you got used to it. As Johnny will testify, Camp coffee is an acquired taste, but once you have acquired it you will never let it go.

The next thing Paterson & Sons needed was a suitable label for the new product. In keeping with their target market, they settled upon an image of a kilted Scottish officer being served Camp coffee by a bewhiskered Indian servant (variously identified as a Punjabi and a Sikh). They chose as the model for the soldier the foremost Scottish warrior of the day, Major-General Sir Hector Macdonald. This was a man who turned down the Victoria Cross in favour of a renewed commission, telling his superiors that he would earn his medal later. Sadly, Macdonald committed suicide in a Paris Hotel room in 1903 after learning that he faced a court martial.

In a reflection of changing attitudes to the colonial era, the Sikh/Punjabi manservant has changed position three times over the years. For the majority of his career, he was portrayed standing holding a bottle of Camp on a silver salver while Macdonald sat enjoying a cuppa. Then, during the 1980s, the tray was dropped. Finally, in 2006, the servant was at last given a chance to

sit down and share a cup of Camp with the officer on equal terms.

The obvious way to use Camp coffee is of course to make pleasingly retro drinks. The classic versions involve combining the liquid essence with hot milk if you want a warming drink and cold milk if you need to cool down. You can also simply use hot water if you are a hardcore fan. But Camp also comes into its own as a baking ingredient. It gives an intense burst of coffee flavour to icing sugar and cake fillings and is so convenient that you would be negligent not to keep a bottle in the larder.

MALTED CAMP COFFEE
MILKSHAKE

Horlicks is a great powdered malted drink that almost made it into our top 17. It is usually imbibed at bedtime, but the Camp coffee in this recipe should ensure that you stay awake. The resulting milkshake is filling, nourishing and leaves you feeling all the better for having consumed it. All you need to make it is a hand blender.

Serves 1

100g good-quality vanilla ice cream

50ml milk

2 teaspoons Camp coffee

1 heaped tablespoon Horlicks (or other malted drink powder)

Blend ingredients together until smooth. This shouldn't take long. Pour into glass. Drink. Make another one.

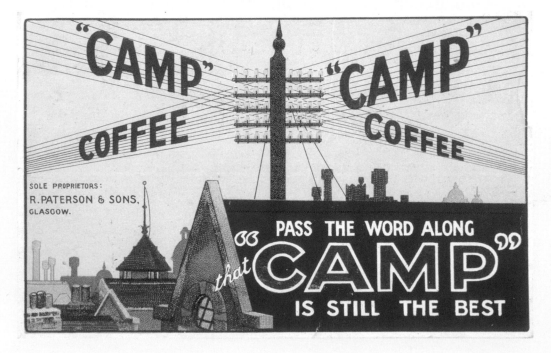

Advertisement on a trade card, 1890s.

CAMP COFFEE FROZEN CRUNCH PIE

This isn't actually a pie but it is frozen and crunchy. It is also embarrassingly easy to make.

Serves 4

- **500ml ice cream (vanilla or chocolate work particularly well)**
- **1 tablespoon Camp coffee**
- **4 meringue nests**

Take the ice cream out of the freezer.

After 10 minutes, by which time the ice cream should have softened, turn it into a bowl.

Pour in the coffee and crumble in the meringues. Stir in until smoothly lumpy bumpy.

Eat some, otherwise it won't fit back into the container. Repackage into the ice cream container and replace in the freezer. Eat when necessary.

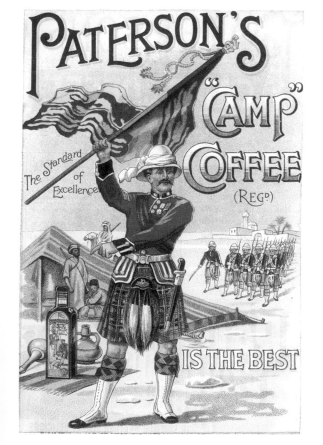

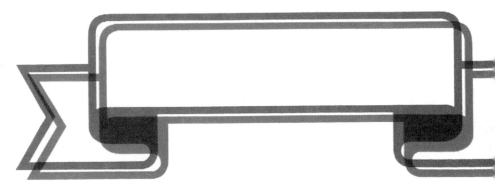

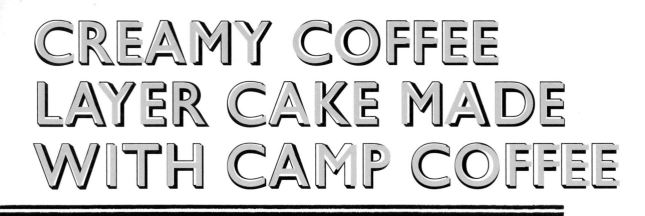

CREAMY COFFEE LAYER CAKE MADE WITH CAMP COFFEE

It's somehow thrilling to base a coffee cake the Women's Institute would be proud of on a product that comes out of a bottle. For this recipe you will need a shallow square oven tin about 30 x 30cm and an electric hand whisk.

Serves 4–6

For the cake

> Butter, for greasing
>
> 4 large eggs
>
> 120g golden caster sugar
>
> Splash of vanilla extract
>
> 100g self-raising flour
>
> 50g ground almonds
>
> 120g clotted cream
>
> 2 tablespoons Camp coffee

For the filling

> 125g Philadelphia cream cheese, at room temperature
>
> 100g unsalted butter, at room temperature
>
> 150g icing sugar
>
> 2 tablespoons Camp coffee
>
> Walnuts or pecans, to decorate

Heat the oven to 180°C/350°F/gas mark 4. Grease the oven tin with butter. Line it with greaseproof paper, pressing it down firmly.

In a large mixing bowl, whisk the eggs and sugar together for 5 minutes until pale and fluffy. Add the vanilla extract.

Sift the flour into the mixture and add the almonds, clotted cream and Camp coffee. Fold all the ingredients together using a spatula. Don't overmix otherwise you will lose all those lovely bubbles.

Don't worry if the clotted cream is still a little lumpy.

Spoon the mixture into the prepared oven tin, spreading it out evenly.

Bake for 15 minutes, until golden brown. Leave to cool in the tin. Once cool, turn it out, face down. Carefully peel off the greaseproof paper.

Cut the cake into 4 squares: these are going to be piled on top of each other to create the layers.

To make the filling, place all the filling ingredients in a large bowl, and whisk together until smooth. You'll need half the mixture to fill the cake and half to cover it.

To assemble the cake, spread a thin layer of filling on top of the first square of cake. Place another layer on top and repeat the process twice more until the top layer is in place.

Trim the sides of the cake with a sharp serrated knife to make it look neat. Spread all over with the filling mixture and decorate with walnuts or pecans.

This cake needs to be refrigerated if you are not eating it on the same day. It will store for up to 5 days in the fridge.

AFOGATO WITH CAMP COFFEE

And now for one of the simplest recipes in the book – a variation on the classic Italian 'coffee over ice cream'. This is for people who don't like espresso but love a little coffee-flavoured indulgence. Serve at the end of a meal.

Serves 1

Take one small, warmed coffee cup... add 1 teaspoon of Camp coffee... top up with boiling water so the cup is one-third full. Add a glistening scoop of ice cream... decorate with a few chocolate sprinkles if the mood takes you... eat immediately!

STICKY TOFFEE TIRAMISU WITH CAMP COFFEE

We're rather proud of our version of tiramisu and believe it would pass muster with the most demanding Italian. The magic of this dish lies in a large saucepan of boiling water. You are going to boil a tin of condensed milk in it for 2½ hours, transforming it into a magical caramel substance which the Argentinians call *dulce de leche*.

This dessert is best made either a day in advance or in the morning if you are serving it for dinner. It needs time in the fridge to set properly.

Serves 4–6

397g tin condensed milk
75ml Camp coffee
75ml dark rum
20 sponge fingers
3 medium eggs, separated
50g caster sugar
300g mascarpone
25g chocolate, grated

You need a large pan of water. In it, you are going to boil the unopened tin of condensed milk. Danger: do not let the saucepan boil dry. If it does, the tin of condensed milk may explode all over your kitchen – much worse than an egg exploding in the microwave! So use the largest saucepan you've got (within reason). Anyway, gently boil the condensed milk for 2½ hours over a low heat with the lid on the saucepan. When the condensed milk is ready, run the tin under the cold tap for a minute or two, then leave to cool.

Add the Camp coffee to the rum and 150ml water, then dip the sponge fingers into it and wedge into the bottom of a medium-size serving dish. Pour any excess coffee over the sodden fingers.

Whisk the egg yolks with the sugar until thick and syrupy. Whisk the egg whites until stiff.

Open the tin of condensed milk and pour into a large bowl. Add the mascarpone and stir until smooth. Fold the egg yolk mixture into the mascarpone mixture, then gently fold in the whisked egg whites. Pour the mixture over the soaked sponge fingers.

Leave to set in the fridge overnight or for the rest of the day; the longer you leave it the more set the tiramisu will be.

Sprinkle with grated chocolate before serving.

Conversion Table

Oven temperatures

Celsius*	Fahrenheit	Gas	Description
110°C	225°F	mark ¼	cool
130°C	250°F	mark ½	cool
140°C	275°F	mark 1	very low
150°C	300°F	mark 2	very low
170°C	325°F	mark 3	low
180°C	350°F	mark 4	moderate
190°C	375°F	mark 5	mod. hot
200°C	400°F	mark 6	hot
220°C	425°F	mark 7	hot
230°C	450°F	mark 8	very hot

* For fan-assisted ovens,
reduce temperatures by 10°C

Length

5mm	¼in
1cm	½in
2cm	¾in
2.5cm	1in
3cm	1¼in
4cm	1½in
5cm	2in
7.5cm	3in
10cm	4in
15cm	6in
18cm	7in
20cm	8in
25cm	10in
28cm	11in
30cm	12in

Weight (solids)

7g	¼oz
10g	½oz
20g	¾oz
25g	1oz
40g	1½oz
50g	2oz
60g	2½oz
75g	3oz
100g	3½oz
110g	4oz (¼lb)
125g	4½oz
150g	5oz
175g	6oz
200g	7oz
225g	8oz (½lb)
250g	9oz
275g	10oz
300g	10½oz
310g	11oz
325g	11½oz
350g	12oz (¾lb)
375g	13oz
400g	14oz
425g	15oz
450g	1lb
500g (½kg)	18oz
600g	1¼lb
700g	1½lb
750g	1lb 10oz
900g	2lb
1kg	2¼lb
1.1kg	2½lb
1.2kg	2lb 12oz
1.3kg	3lb
1.5kg	3lb 5oz
1.6kg	3½lb
1.8kg	4lb
2kg	4½lb
2.25kg	5lb
2.5kg	5lb 8oz
3kg	6lb 8oz

Volume (liquids)

5ml	1 teaspoon
10ml	1 dessertspoon
15ml	1 tablespoon or ½fl oz
30ml	1fl oz
40ml	1½fl oz
50ml	2fl oz
60ml	2½fl oz
75ml	3fl oz
100ml	3½fl oz
125ml	4fl oz
150ml	5fl oz (¼ pint)
160ml	5½fl oz
175ml	6fl oz
200ml	7fl oz
225ml	8fl oz
250ml (0.25 litre)	9fl oz
300ml	10fl oz (½ pint)
325ml	11fl oz
350ml	12fl oz
370ml	13fl oz
400ml	14fl oz
425ml	15fl oz (¾ pint)
450ml	16fl oz
500ml (0.5 litre)	18fl oz
550ml	19fl oz
600ml	20fl oz (1 pint)
700ml	1¼ pints
850ml	1½ pints
1 litre	1¾ pints
1.2 litres	2 pints
1.5 litres	2½ pints
1.8 litres	3 pints
2 litres	3½ pints

Index

Acknowledgements

Kellogg's cornflakes is a registered trademark of Kellogg's NA Company.

Quaker oats is a registered trademark of PepsiCo Beverages & Foods.

Nutella is a registered trademark of Ferrero.

Colman's/Hellmann's/Marmite image is used with kind permission of Unilever.

Skippy® is a registered trademark.

Vegemite and Philadelphia cream cheese are registered trademarks of Kraft Foods Limited.

Heinz tomato ketchup, Heinz baked beans and Lea & Perrins Worcestershire sauce are trademarked copyrighted materials and owned exclusively by H.J. Heinz Company and its affiliates.

TABASCO® is a registered trademark; the TABASCO bottle design and label designs are the exclusive property of McIlhenny Company, Avery Island, LA USA 70513.
www.TABASCO.com

Kikkoman soy sauce is a registered trademark of Kikkoman Trading Europe.

The GUINNESS word and associated logos are trademarks.

Coca-Cola is a registered trademark of the Coca-Cola Company.

Camp coffee is a registered trademark of McCormick (UK) Limited.

PICTURE CREDITS
All photography by Jonathan Gregson except for the following:
Page 6 Mary Evans Picture Library / Alamy; 13 Image courtesy of The Advertising Archives; 14 Image courtesy of Kellogg's; 18 Image courtesy of Kellogg's; 22 Mary Evans Picture Library; 34 Advertisement by McCann Erickson Puerto Rico; 49 Image courtesy of The Advertising Archives; 59 Mary Evans Picture Library / Alamy; 62 Image courtesy of The Advertising Archives; 65 The History of Advertising Trust; 76 Image courtesy of The Advertising Archives; 78 Image courtesy of Unilever Archives; 80 Image courtesy of Unilever Archives; 90 Image courtesy of The Advertising Archives; 100 The History of Advertising Trust; 103 The History of Advertising Trust; 108 The History of Advertising Trust; 109 The History of Advertising Trust; 116 Image courtesy of The Advertising Archives; 130 Image courtesy of Kikkoman; 133 Mary Evans Picture Library; 137 Mary Evans Picture Library; 143 GL Archive / Alamy; 144 Antiques & Collectables / Alamy; 152 Mary Evans Picture Library; 153 Mary Evans Picture Library / Alamy

The HJ Heinz Co Ltd Archive held at the History of Advertising Trust:
http://www.hatads.org.uk

Illustration on page 5 by David Juniper.

Product shots on pages 33 and 45 by Jake Tilson.

TV advert on page 49 by JWT (J Walter Thompson), starring the actress Sara Crowe.

TYPOGRAPHY
Typeset in Industria Inline designed by Neville Brody, Clarendon designed by Hermann Eidenbenz, Gill Sans Shadowed designed by Eric Gill, Interstate designed by Tobias Frere-Jones.

AUTHORS' ACKNOWLEDGEMENTS
Thanks to the food team at Pret, a truly cool brand. (NS)